Omnia vincit Amor, et nos cedamus Amori! —Vergil

Patricia Reinhart

Verlag für moderne Kunst

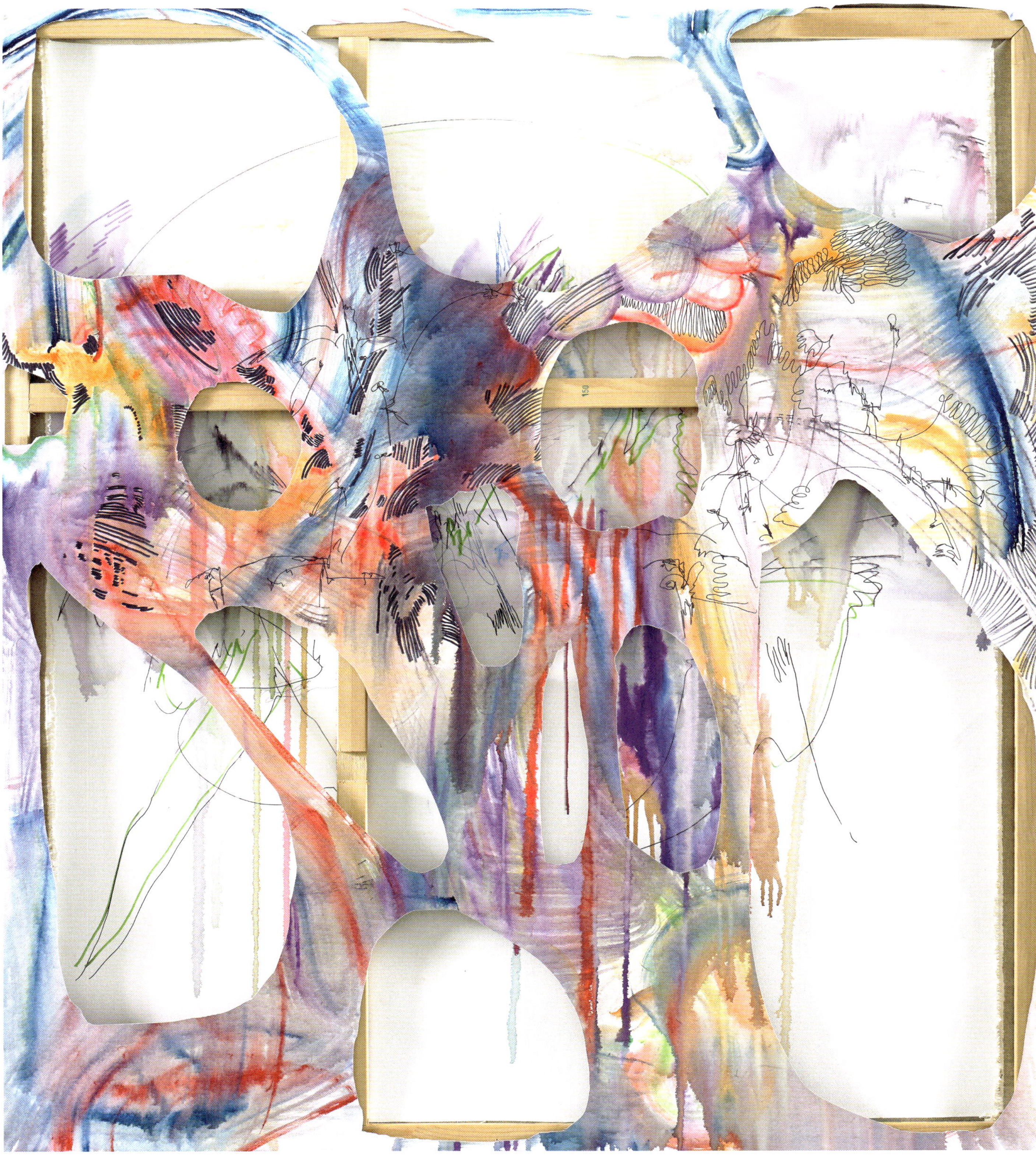

Untitled (NM), mixed media on canvas, 170 × 150 × 5 cm, 2021

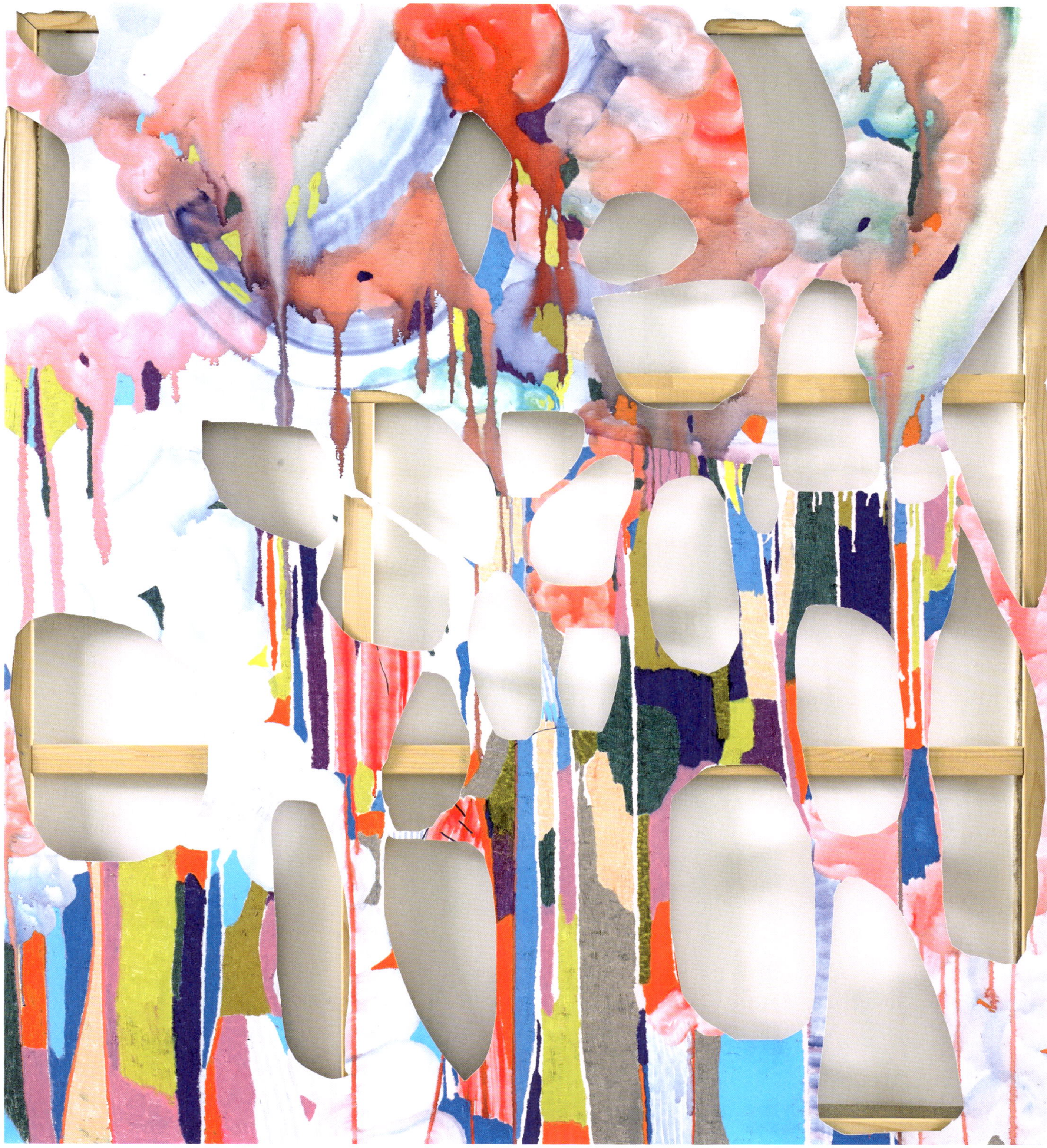

Coïncidences III, watercolour/oil pastel on linen, 170 × 150 cm, 2021

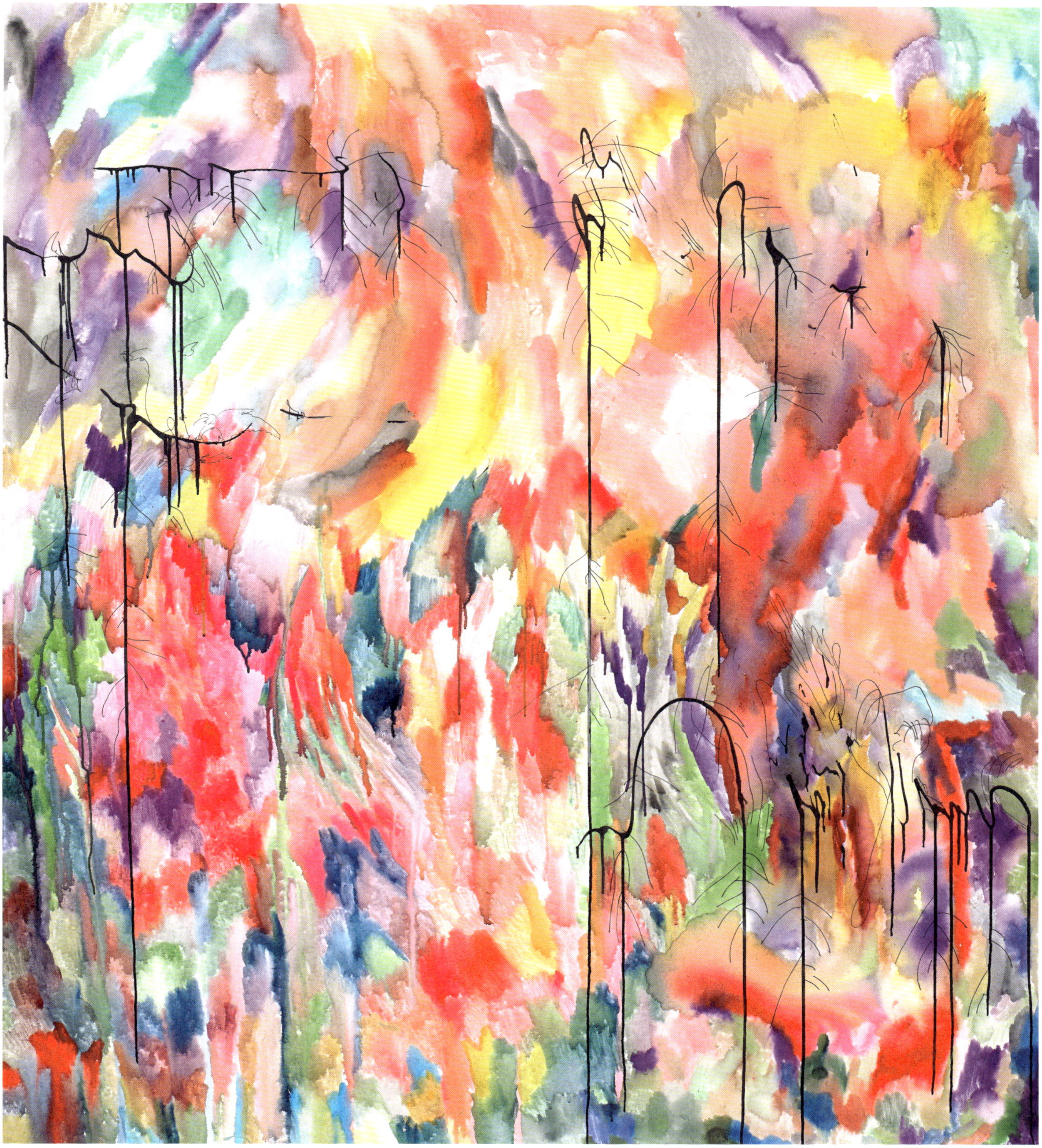

XXV – W VI (Sleep 5/3), watercolour/marker on linen, 170 × 150 cm, 2021

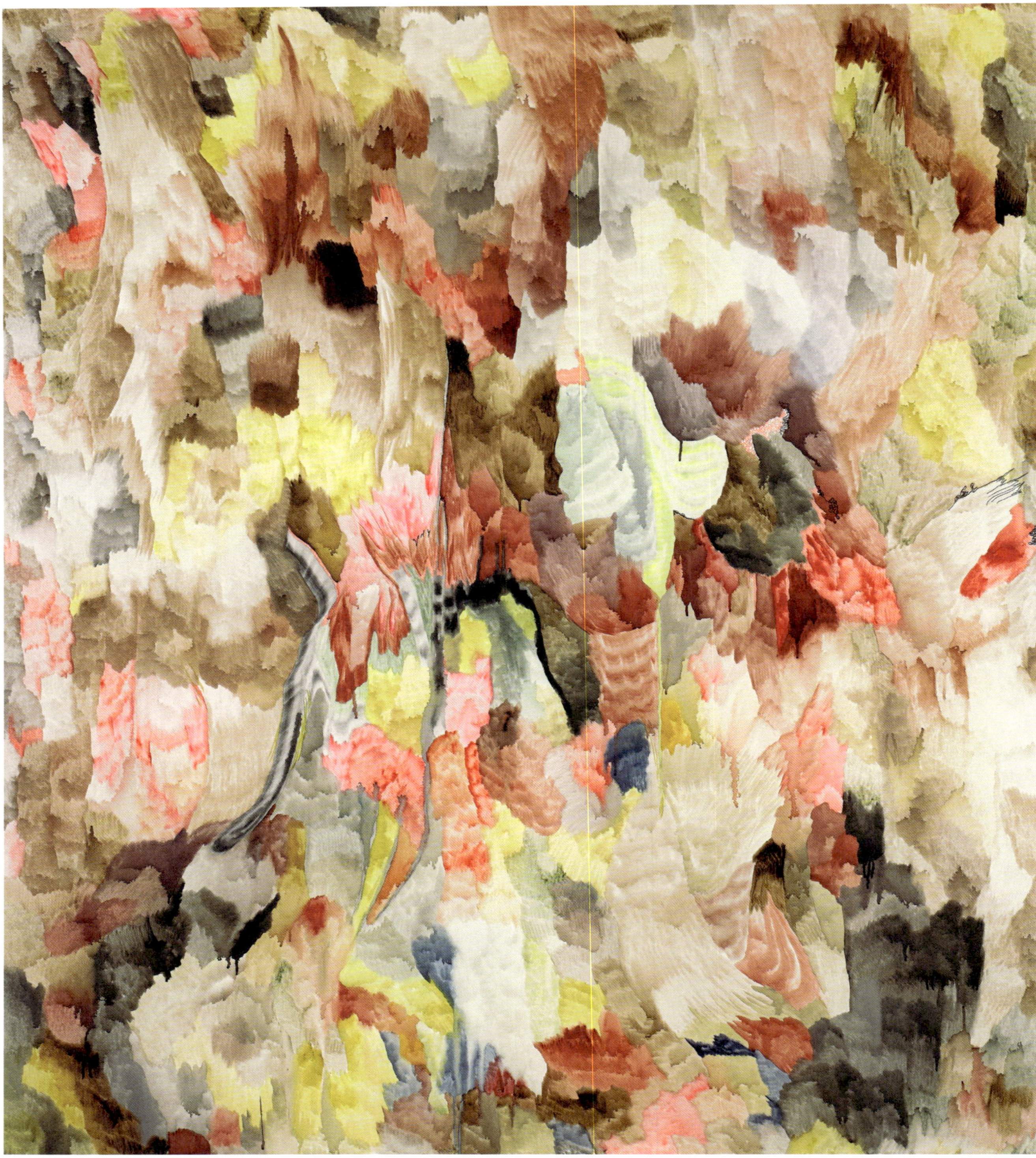

Patience XV – Über die Notwendigkeit des Zerschmetterns, watercolour/marker on linen, 170 × 150 cm, 2016

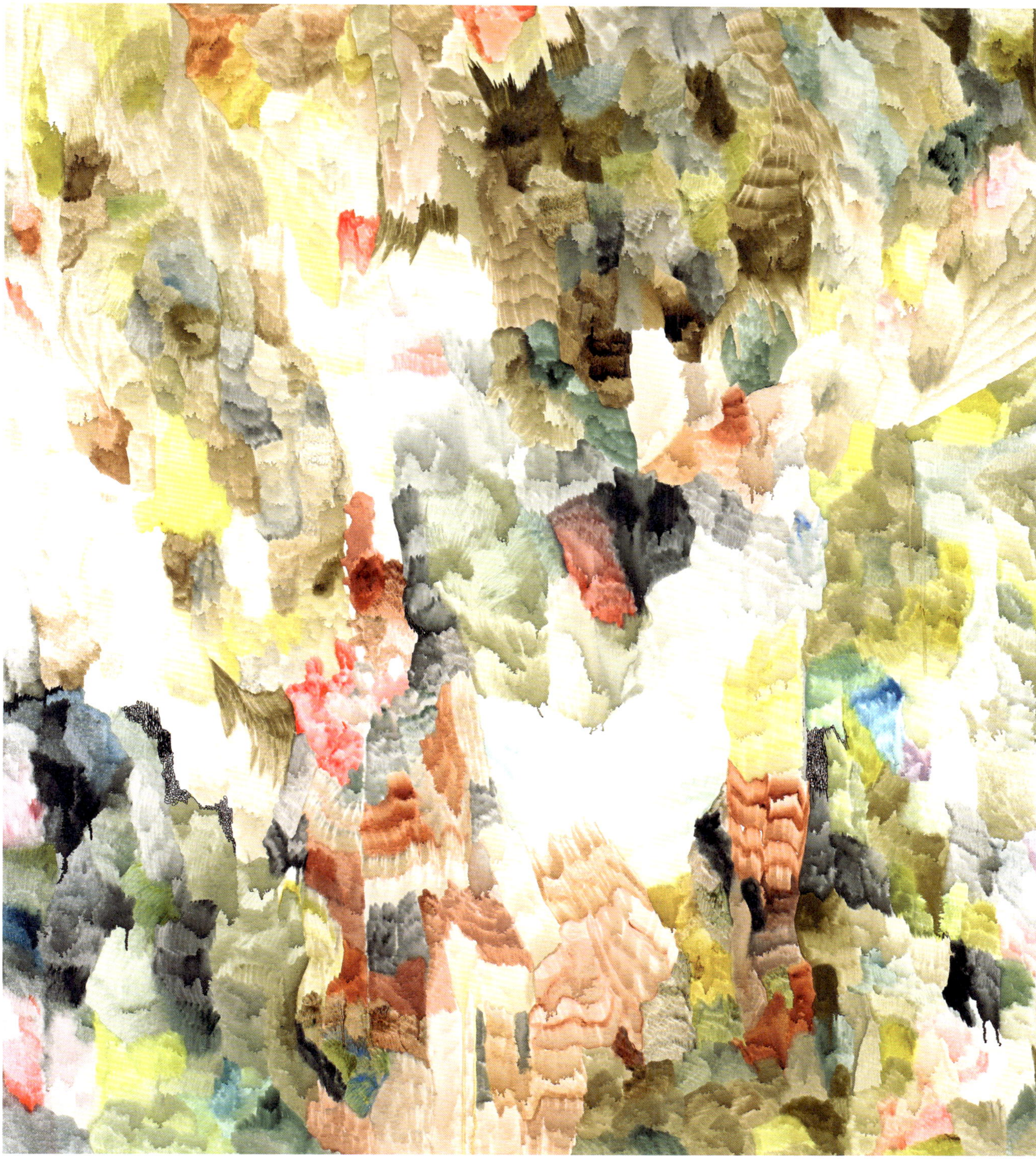

Patience XIV – Attitude / Das weibliche Rückgrat, watercolour/marker on l nen, 170 × 150 cm, 2016

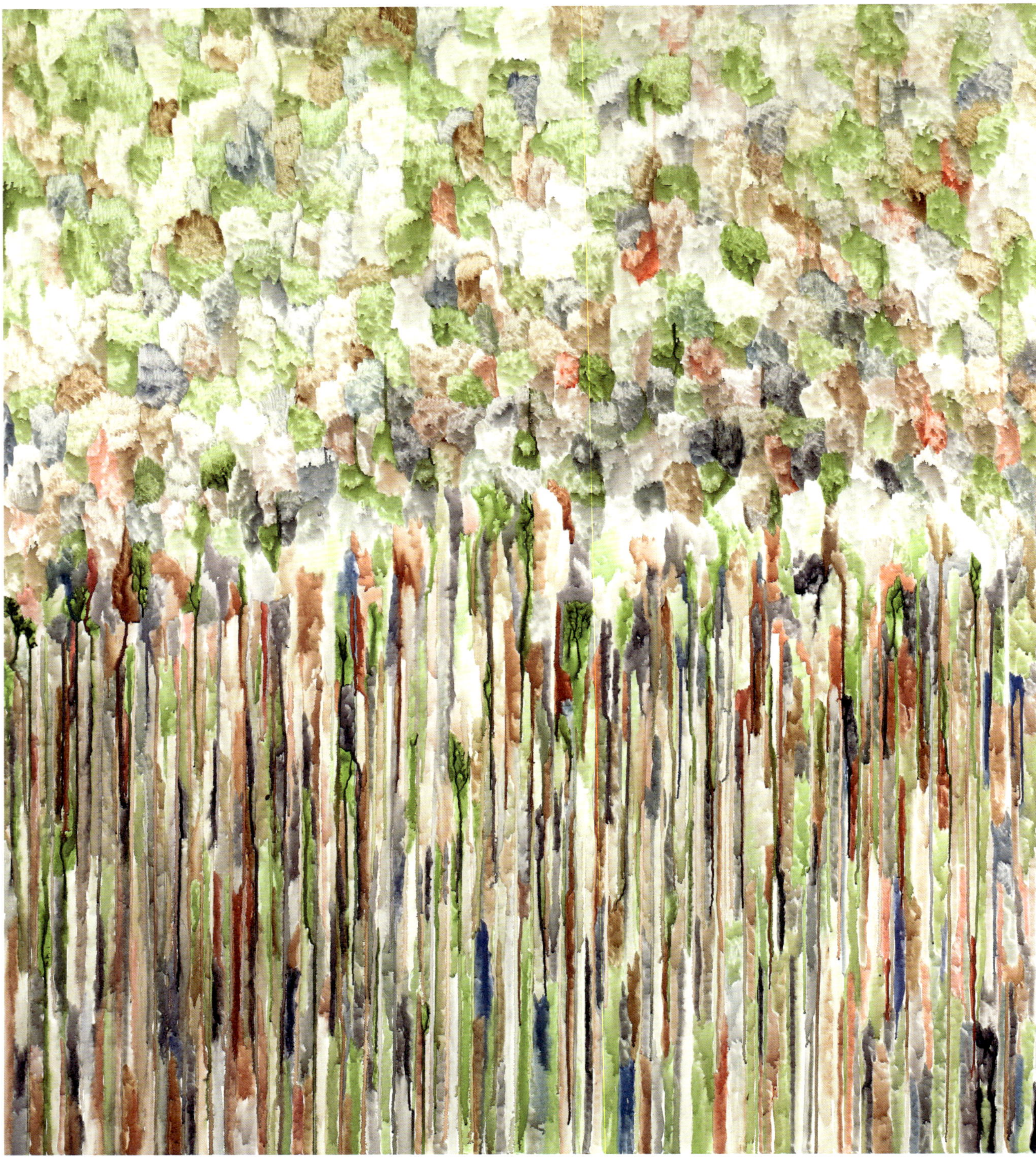

Patience II – La forêt et le ciel (Irony), watercolour on linen, 170 × 150 cm, 2015

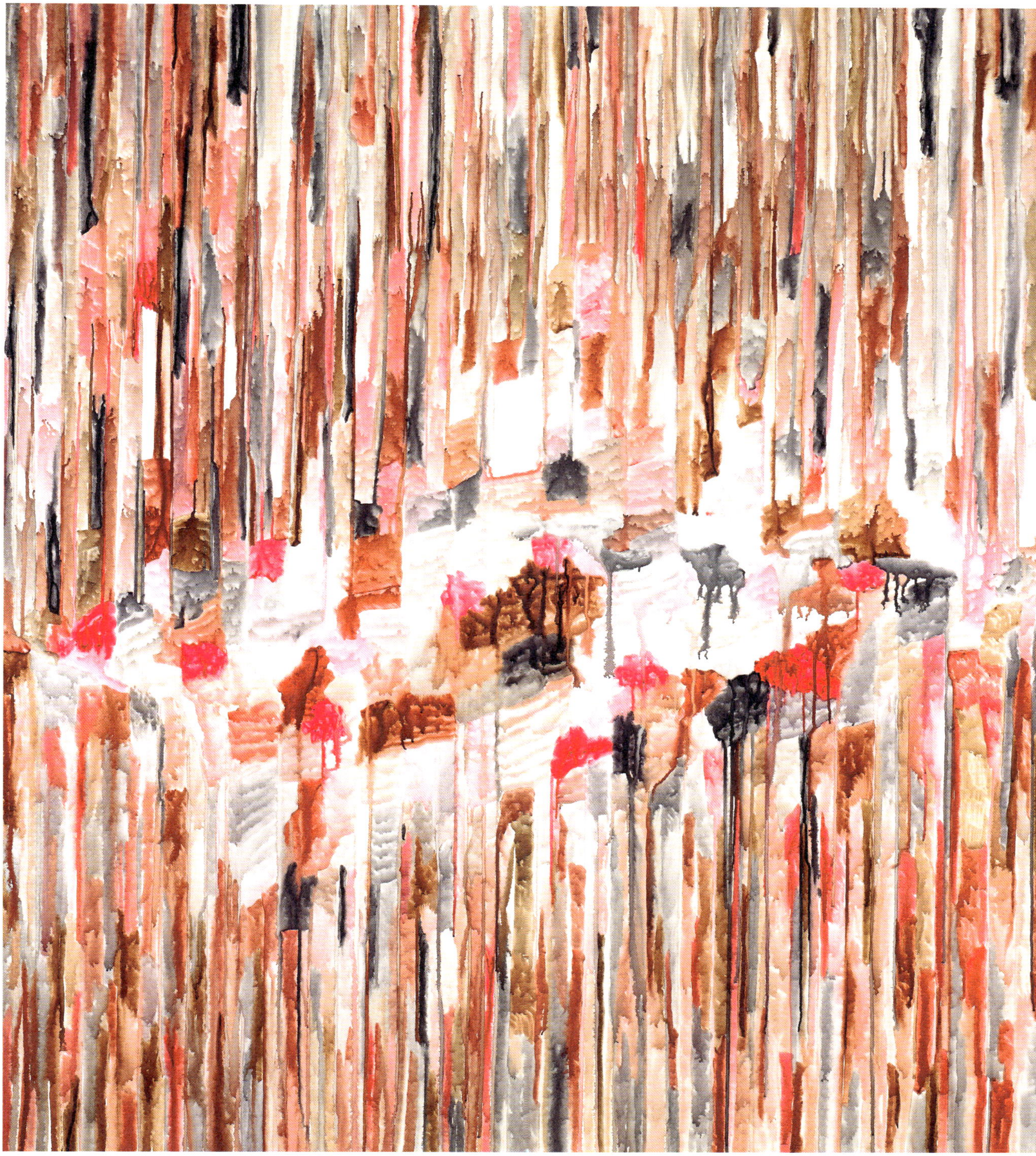

Patience III – L'amour, watercolour on linen, 170 × 150 cm, 2015

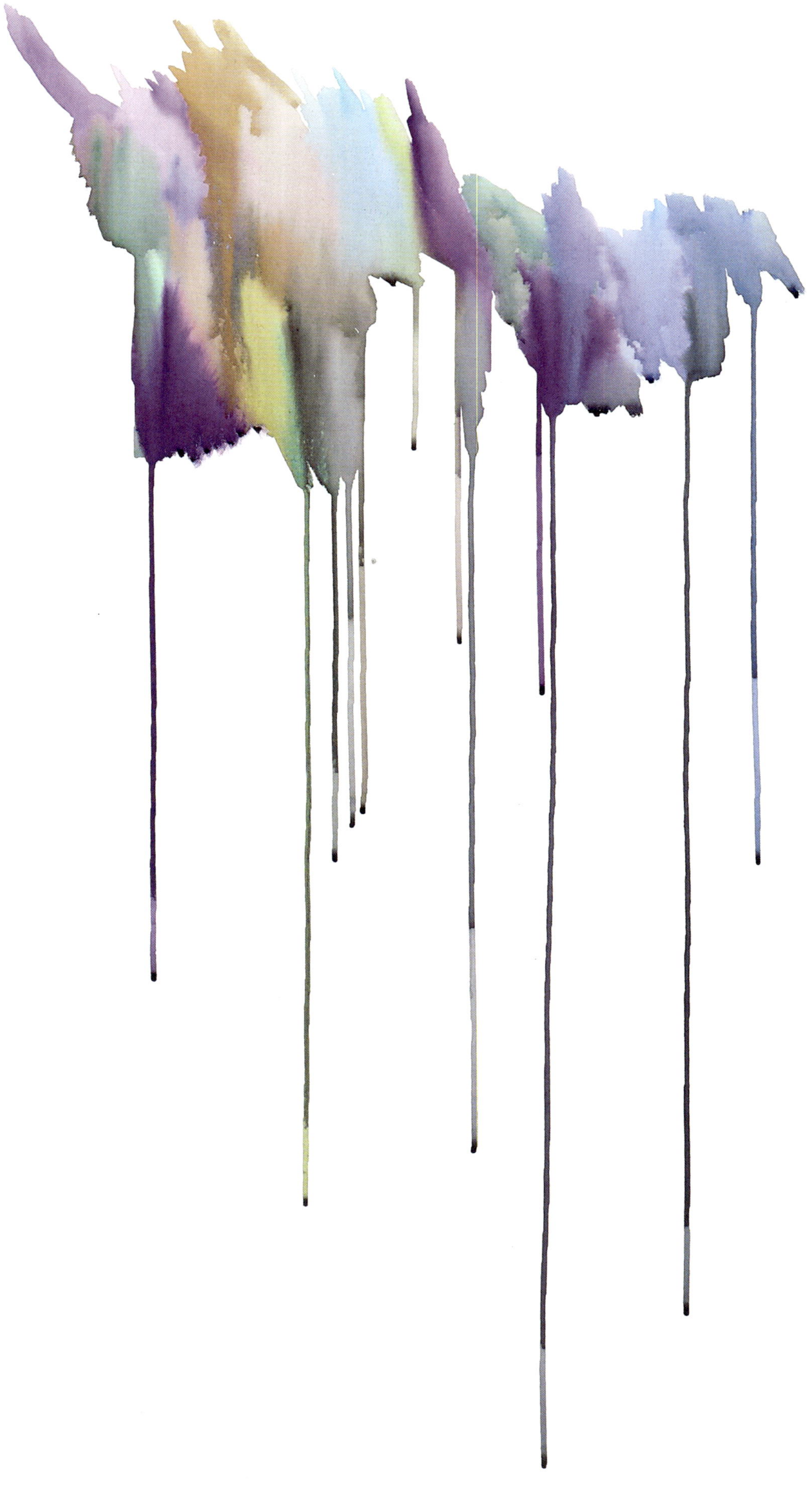

Kaleidoscope and Cosmos Of Abstractions in Painting

Synne Genzmer

> *... taking a certain definite line of action and staying with it.*[1] —Georgia O'Keeffe

> *Exploring the universe has brought a new dimension. [...] Einstein's discovery of the cosmos is the infinite dimension, without end. And so we have here: Foreground, middle ground, background. [...] how can this be taken further, what would I have to do? [...] I make holes, infinity passes through them, light passes through them; there is no need to paint.*[2] —Lucio Fontana

In the 20th century, purposely perforating or damaging the canvas became a means of expression and a symbolic gesture. It elevated the violent and destructive to an aesthetic element, but also stood for a reaching-out into new dimensions, simultaneously emphasising the presence of the real and the metaphorical in painting: Niki de Saint Phalle shot her reliefs in an emancipatory act, Joan Miró presented *Burnt Canvases* as a protest against political oppression and the reduction of art to a commodity for an elitist society. Finally, Lucio Fontana ventured to expand the limiting area of the canvas with his *Concetto spaziale* and open it up to infinite space.

These artists worked – each in their own way – with a negative surface, a literally empty space, which – in the form of holes, perforations, cuts or cut-out surfaces – acquires creative power, not only represented, but actually present. In her *Cut-Outs,* Patricia Reinhart uses the cut as a precisely-calculated technique that does not destroy the painted forms of her pictures, rather imitates them. She cuts into or out of compositions in a controlled and precise way, using the knife like a scalpel for correction. The art of painting becomes sculptural at this moment, its fragility disturbed. It resembles making a sculpture out of the canvas when the artist takes out those parts of the painting, like taking them out of a body. They need to be removed in order for the painting to function. Glimpses and lines of sight emerge onto something behind, onto the wall behind the canvas or into another room; as "sandwich paintings" they are layers that double the painted space as a painting in front of the painting. Many *Cut-Outs* make the stretcher frame visible on which the canvas, which is only present in narrow sections, is mounted. In front of the wall, the *Cut-Outs* cast shadows, they create optical effects like shapes, so that the illusion of painting, which requires a uniform surface, is disrupted by real space.

In her early years, Patricia Reinhart used the painting medium for sketches and preliminary drawings in a figurative way, parallel to her silent films, in which she thematized the role of women in various cultural/historical settings and according to literary models, as in *Untitled* (2007). This confrontation also influenced some of her oil pastels from 2012 and 2013, in which the theme of the garden is echoed when the surface is filled with vegetal forms and nature becomes ornament. In the work *Untitled* (2014), there is an affinity with plant forms in Matisse's work, which were painted first, then reappeared as cut-outs in the modernist painter's work and migrated as cut out paper from the canvas directly to the walls of his studio. Viewing painting as a space whose abstract structures derive from a garden leads directly to Monet's *Nymphéas.* As a permanent installation at the Musée de l'Orangerie in Paris, the canvas virtually nestles up against the oval walls, overlaps with the presentation space, becoming indistinguishable from it. The areas of colour spots, which from a distance project a carpet of water lilies onto our retinas, anticipate the abstractions that characterise the works of Jackson Pollock. By creating an installation, the garden is brought indoors, blurring inside and outside, turning the gallery into an illusionistic landscape that unfolds along its walls. A garden is also the setting for Reinhart's film work *Anoir and the Woman in the Garden* (2015–2017), in which a female protagonist dressed in white moves through a scenery of lush, exotic plants. The pool of water in the centre, in which nature and sky are reflected, appears like the cinematic mirror of abstract painting

Detail *Untitled*, watercolour on linen, 170 × 150 cm, 2018

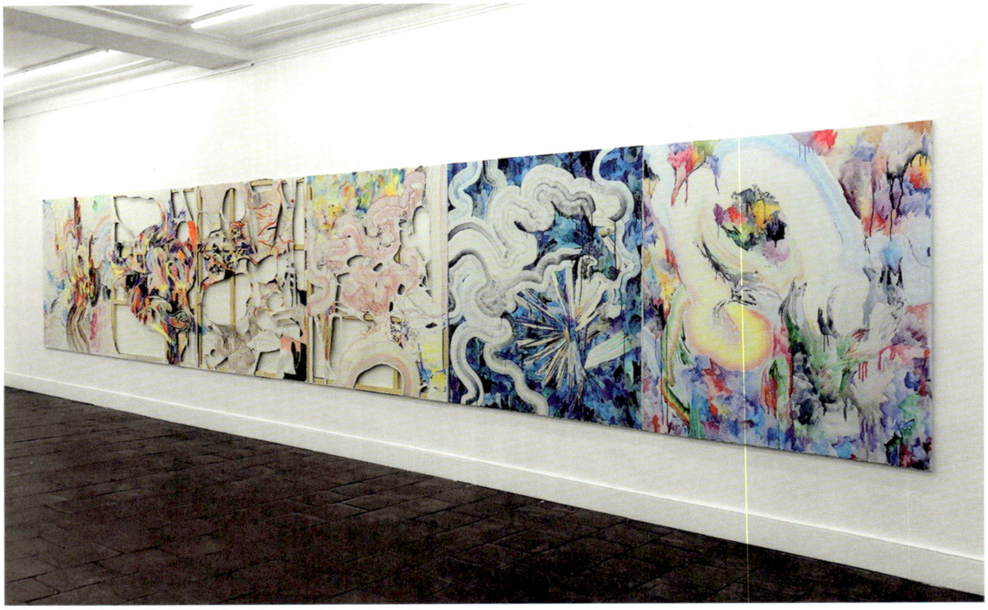

Exhibition view / Ausstellungsansicht / Vue de l'exposition *In Bloom*, Galerie Mansart, Paris, 2019

and its landscape-like impression, attributable to Patricia Reinhart's painting. The garden possesses strong symbolic meaning as a symbol of its own, female space, which underlines the artist's attitude and her strong awareness of being a female painter, of occupying a role as a woman in a contemporary way, representing with verve this space which has been historically dominated by men for so long.

The beginning of an extended stay in Paris coincided with a discovery of watercolours, which replaced the intense, expressionistic painting in oil on canvas soaked in turpentine. With a specific glazing style of painting that emphasised and used the watery, the fluid, the fluidity of colour, new pictorial dimensions emerged as themes and structural elements, bringing with them a distinct turn towards abstraction. Whereas Patricia Reinhart had previously worked most often with oil pastels, which led to themes oscillating between the figurative and the abstract, she soon began to eschew the figurative form in her watercolours. An affinity with narrative or representational depictions that can be discovered in abstract forms or lie hidden beneath them are, however, still present in many paintings, yet it becomes a testimony to an interest in phenomena that can be grasped in a less representationally limited way, promoting insights into the effects of forces and energies. For example, they show a whirlwind of colours and shapes energetically illustrating a thunderstorm, rather than depicting the observable version of this natural phenomenon.

Patricia Reinhart does not use watercolours in a conventional manner. Rather, her specific production method consciously incorporates the flowing properties of watercolour, such as the running and trickling down of the paint or its surface-like spread, into compositions created intuitively and without preliminary drawings directly onto the blank canvas, employing them to create certain aesthetic formations. This technique also seemed suitable for the representability of inner, unconscious and emotional processes and spaces. Works such as *XXV – W VI (Sleep 5/3)* (2021) or *Cut-Out / Lucid Dream* (2018) betray an inspiration from the field of psychoanalysis. A visualisation of psychic structures is not programmatically artistic, but part of a self-referential search for the truthful, the authentic, the metaphysical – a form of meditation characterised by authenticity: "The stroke is real, it has its own tension, and it is an intimate act of painting",[3] says the artist. The colour orgies of her paintings radiate a sensuality that is at once powerful and delicate, combining small-scale forms into larger dynamic patterns of movement. They are forces rather than calculated formations. They also reflect the artist's interest in colour materiality, its varying density, its properties and possibilities of articulation, its non-illusionistic roughness, its sensitivity associated with femininity. Patricia Reinhart uses the entire colour spectrum, which manifests inherent principles of optics and physics, transforming the work into a painterly space of experience within which we are encouraged to dream.

Abstract colour/form structures can be interpreted as expandable inner space and as the idea of a cosmic space that points to an infinite vastness. Their respective sections can be continued infinitely, since they are not limited by the representational. Such a "surveying of the world", as Patricia Reinhart has called a series of paintings (*NM*, 2020–2022), visualises itself abstractly as an expression of imagination. Depth of space is created by layers of light-dark contrasts

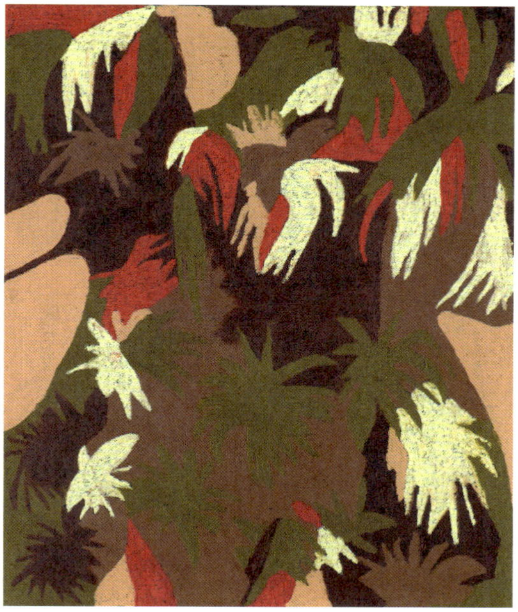

Untitled, oil pastel on linen, 60 × 50 cm, 2014

formed by a staggered juxtaposition and superimposition of delicate and strong colours, i.e. thinner or thicker applications of paint in different formations. Drawn elements crisscross the polymorphous colour structures and are reminiscent of circles, diagrammatic fragments or spatial markings. Bubbling skies, fireworks, explosions, storms or energies in constant flux as visualisations of inner states suggest that the infinity of space can be experienced inwardly rather than through an objective view. It is true that we sense an infinite space when looking toward the horizon at sea, in the clear night sky or when flying above the clouds. Since infinity does not permit an all-encompassing view, we can only grasp this space visually as a fragment or symbol. Painted infinity spans a symbolic space on the canvas, the extension of which is left to the imagination. One familiar cultural symbol for a material and mental, psychic or spiritual space that is doubly imagined in this way is the heavenly paradise, which, on Earth, manifests as a garden. Patricia Reinhart's series *Paradise I–III* (2018–2020) is dedicated to this construct.

As demonstrated by important artists of the 20th century from Hilma af Klint, Piet Mondrian and Kazimir Malevich to Lee Krasner, the history of abstract painting is permeated by an understanding of non-representational compositions as representative of spiritual dimensions. Patricia Reinhart's multi-part series *Coïncidences* (2021/22) or *Patience* (2015/16) are conceived as analogies between abstract forms and abstract concepts of space, time and encounter. Colour in particular, condensed through its properties into materiality, establishes close relationships between material and non-material worlds. Colour can be a starting point for considerations on a physical, neurological or psychological level that breach inner and outer spaces alike. It guides us into the realm of mysticism on a cultural level or into quantum physics on a scientific level. As subjective expression, Patricia Reinhart's painting approaches those superordinate laws inscribed on the world, even as its form aesthetically links it to non-visible aspects of human existence.

Synne Genzmer works as a freelance curator and writer. Studied Art History at the University of Vienna. 2007–2012 in the curatorial team of the Kunsthalle Wien. 2013/14 Manager of Publications, Generali Foundation, Vienna.

1 Georgia O'Keeffe, in: David W. Galenson, *Conceptual Revolutions in Twentieth-Century Art*, Cambridge 2009, p. 97, translation by the author.
2 Lucio Fontana, in: Carla Lonzi, *Autoritratto. Accardi, Alviani, Castellani, Consagra, Fabro, Fontana, Kounellis, Nigro, Paolini, Pascali, Rotella, Scarpitta, Turcato, Twombly*, Bari 1969, p. 169–171, translation by the author.
3 Patricia Reinhart in conversation in November 2021.

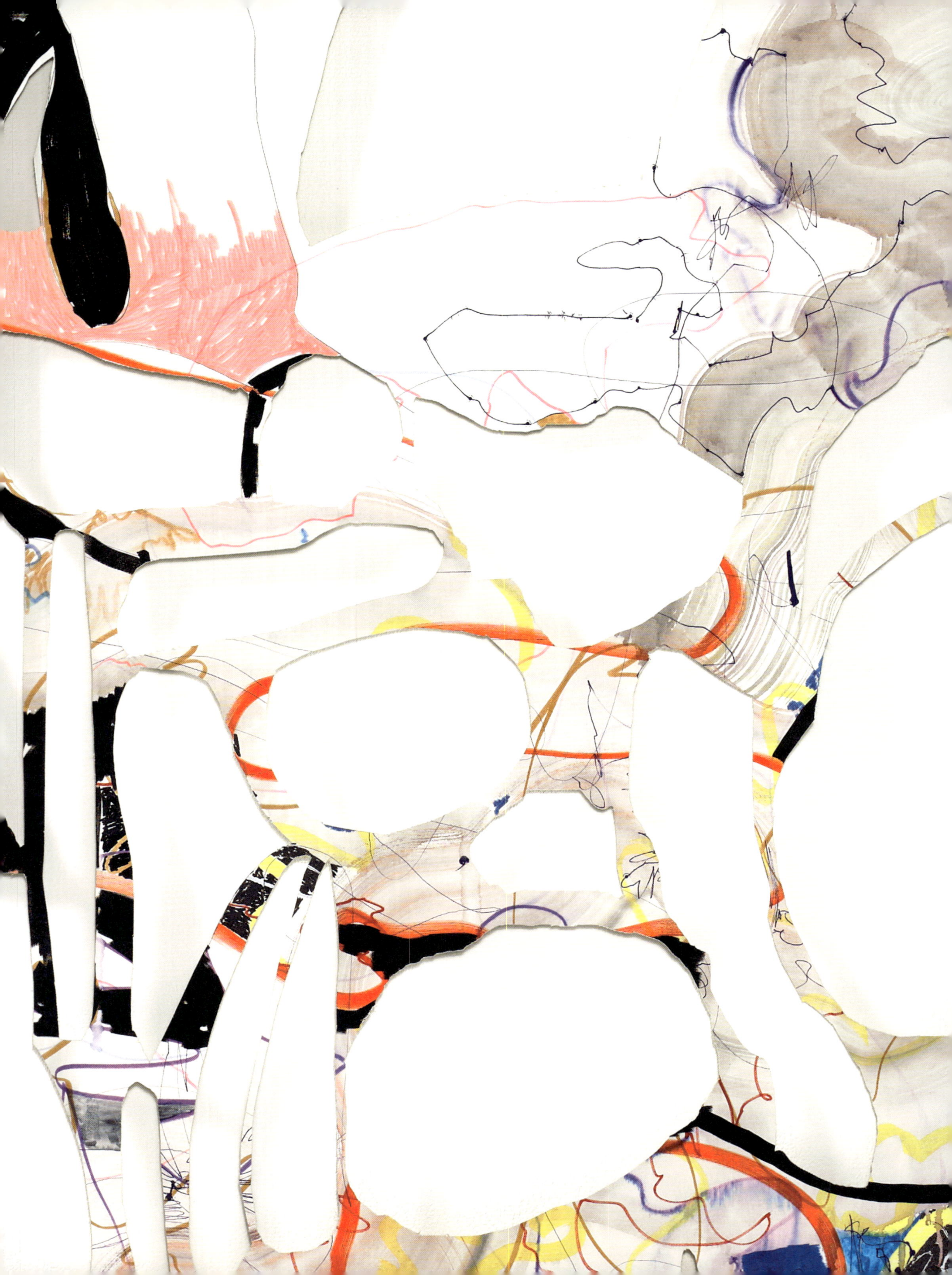

Kaleidoskop und Kosmos
Von Abstraktionen in der Malerei

Synne Genzmer

> *… sich für eine bestimmte Vorgehensweise zu entscheiden und diese beizubehalten.*[1] —Georgia O'Keeffe

> *Die Entdeckung des Kosmos ist eine neue Dimension. […] Einsteins Entdeckung des Kosmos ist die unendliche Dimension, ohne Ende.*
> *Und so haben wir hier: Vordergrund, Mittelgrund und Hintergrund. […] Um weiterzugehen, was muss ich tun? […] Ich mache Löcher, die Unendlichkeit geht durch sie hindurch, das Licht geht durch sie hindurch, man braucht nicht zu malen.*[2] —Lucio Fontana

Die Perforierung oder Verletzung der Leinwand wurde im 20. Jahrhundert zu einem Gestaltungsmittel und einer symbolischen Geste, erhob das Gewaltvolle und Zerstörerische zum ästhetischen Element, stand aber auch für ein Vorstoßen zu neuen Dimensionen und betonte zugleich das Reale und das Metaphorische der Malerei: Niki de Saint Phalle schoss in einem emanzipatorischen Akt auf ihre Reliefs, Joan Miró präsentierte seine *Burnt Canvases* als Protest gegen politische Unterdrückung und die Reduzierung der Kunst zu einer Ware für eine elitäre Gesellschaft. Lucio Fontana schließlich wollte mit seinem *Concetto spaziale* den Raum der Leinwand erweitern und zum unendlichen Raum hin öffnen.

Auf unterschiedliche Weisen arbeiteten die Künstler:innen mit einer negativen Fläche, einem buchstäblich leeren Raum, der – in Form von Löchern, Durchbohrungen, Schnitten oder ausgeschnittenen Flächen – gestalterische Kraft bekommt, jedoch nicht repräsentiert wird, sondern tatsächlich vorhanden ist. Patricia Reinhart setzt in ihren *Cut-Outs* den Schnitt als präzises Werkzeug ein, der die gemalten Formen ihrer Bilder nicht zerstört, sondern nachahmt. Sie schneidet kontrolliert und genau in Kompositionen hinein oder etwas aus ihnen heraus, benutzt das Messer wie ein Skalpell zur Korrektur. Malerei wird in diesem Moment skulptural, ihre Fragilität gestört. Es ist wie ein Skulptieren der Leinwand, wenn die Künstlerin aus dem Gemälde wie aus einem Körper jene Teile herausoperiert, die notwendigerweise entfernt werden müssen, damit das Bild funktioniert. Es entstehen Durchblicke und Blickachsen auf ein Dahinter, auf die Wand hinter der Leinwand oder in einen anderen Raum; als „Sandwich Paintings" sind es Schichten, die als Gemälde vor dem Gemälde den gemalten Raum verdoppeln. Viele *Cut-Outs* lassen den Keilrahmen sichtbar werden, auf dem die nur noch in schmalen Teilen vorhandene Leinwand aufgespannt ist. Auf die Wand werfen die *Cut-Outs* Schatten, sie erzeugen optisch körperhafte Effekte, sodass die Illusion der Malerei, die einer einheitlichen Fläche bedarf, durch den realen Raum gebrochen wird.

In frühen Jahren setzte Patricia Reinhart das malerische Medium für Skizzen und Vorzeichnungen in figurativer Weise parallel zu ihren Stummfilmen ein, in denen sie die Rolle der Frau in unterschiedlichen kulturgeschichtlichen Prägungen und nach literarischen Vorlagen thematisierte (*Untitled*, 2007). Diese Auseinandersetzung prägte ebenso einige ihrer Ölpastelle aus den Jahren 2012 und 2013. Darin klingt auch das Motiv des Gartens an, wenn die Fläche mit vegetabilen Formen ausgefüllt wird und die Natur zum Ornament gerät. In der Arbeit *Untitled* (2014) ist eine Ähnlichkeit zu den Pflanzenformen bei Matisse zu erkennen, die zuerst gemalt, dann als Cut-outs im Werk des Malers zu finden sind und als ausgeschnittenes Papier von der Leinwand direkt an die Wände seines Ateliers gewandert sind. Die Malerei als einen Raum zu betrachten, dessen abstrakte Strukturen sich von einem Garten ableiten, führt zu den *Nymphéas* Monets. Als permanente Installation im Musée de l'Orangerie in Paris schmiegt sich die Leinwand an die ovalen Wände, überlagert sich mit dem Raum der Präsentation, wird von ihm ununterscheidbar. Die Flächen aus Farbflecken, die aus der Distanz auf unserer Netzhaut zu einem Seerosenteppich werden, nehmen das abstrakte All-over eines Jackson Pollock vorweg. Durch die Rauminstallation wird der Garten in den Innenraum geholt, lässt das Innen und das Außen miteinander verschwimmen, macht die Galerie zu einer illusionistischen Landschaft, die sich entlang

Detail *Cut-Out*, watercolour/acryl/marker on linen, 170 × 150 cm, 2017

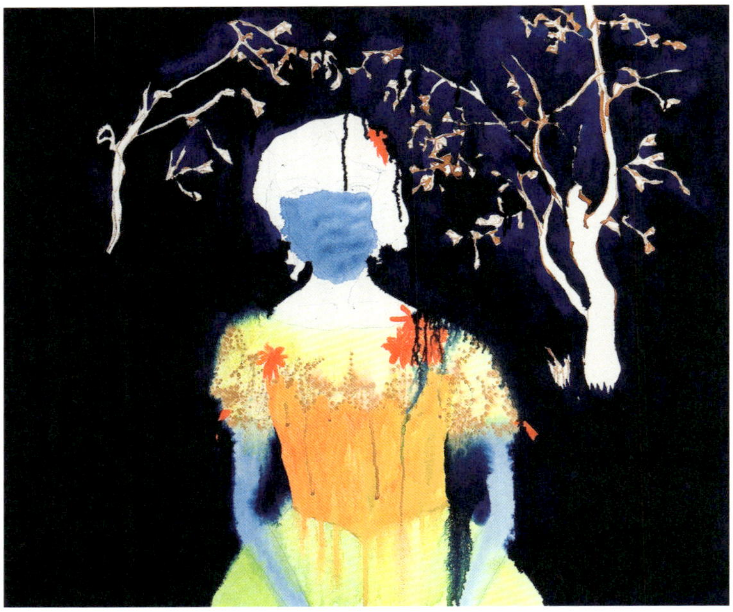

Untitled, oil/marker on linen, 60 × 71 cm, 2007

der Wände entfaltet. Ein Garten ist auch das Setting für Reinharts Filmarbeit *Anoir and the Woman in the Garden* (2015–2017), in dem sich eine in Weiß gekleidete Protagonistin durch eine Szenerie voller üppiger exotischer Pflanzen bewegt. Das Wasserbecken im Zentrum, in dem sich Natur und Himmel spiegeln, erscheint wie der filmische Spiegel abstrakter Malerei und ihrer landschaftlichen Anmutung, die dem malerischen Schaffen von Patricia Reinhart zugeschrieben werden kann. Der Garten hat als Sinnbild eines eigenen, weiblichen Raumes eine starke symbolische Bedeutung, die die Haltung der Künstlerin unterstreicht, ebenso wie ihr starkes Bewusstsein dafür, eine Malerin zu sein und als Frau eine Rolle, die historisch sehr lange männlich dominiert war, zeitgenössisch zu besetzen und mit Verve zu vertreten.

Der Beginn eines mehrjährigen Aufenthaltes in Paris fiel für Patricia Reinhart zusammen mit der Entdeckung von Aquarellfarben, die das intensive, expressionistische und in Terpentin getränkte Malen in Öl auf Leinwand ablösten. Mit einer spezifischen lasierenden Malweise, die das Wässrige, Flüssige, Fließende der Farben betonte und nutzte, entstanden motivisch und strukturell neue piktorale Dimensionen, die eine Hinwendung zur Abstraktion mit sich brachten. Hatte Patricia Reinhart zuvor oftmals mit Ölkreide und zwischen Figurativem und Abstraktion oszillierenden Motiven gearbeitet, löste sie sich mit der Aquarellfarbe von figurativen Formen. Eine Affinität zu narrativen oder gegenständlichen Darstellungen, die sich in abstrakten Formen entdecken lassen oder darunter verborgen liegen, ist jedoch in vielen Gemälden – das zeigen ihre Benennungen – noch präsent. Deutlich wird aber das Interesse an Phänomenen, die nicht so sehr gegenständlich begrenzt erfasst werden können, sondern als Auswirkungen von Kräften und Energien sichtbar werden. Sie zeigen beispielsweise einen Wirbelsturm der Farben und Formen, die ein Gewitter energetisch beschreiben, nicht aber als ein Naturphänomen, das beobachtet werden kann.

Aquarellfarben verwendet Patricia Reinhart nicht in den typischen Techniken. Ihre spezifische Arbeitsweise bezieht aber jene fließenden Eigenschaften der Aquarellfarbe, wie das Verlaufen und Herunterrinnen der Farbe oder ihre flächenhafte Ausbreitung, bewusst in die intuitiv und ohne Vorzeichnungen direkt auf der weißen Leinwand entstehenden Kompositionen mit ein und nutzt sie für bestimmte ästhetische Formationen. Diese Technik erschien auch für die Darstellbarkeit von inneren, unbewussten und emotionalen Vorgängen und Räumen geeignet. Arbeiten wie *XXV – W VI (Sleep 5/3)* (2021) oder *Cut-Out / Lucid Dream* (2018) verraten, dass sie durch die Psychoanalyse inspiriert sind. Eine Visualisierung psychischer Strukturen ist kein künstlerisches Programm, sondern Teil einer das eigene Selbst betreffenden Suche nach dem Wahrhaftigen, Authentischen, Metaphysischen und eine Form der Meditation, die sich durch Echtheit auszeichnet: „Der Strich ist echt, er hat seine eigene Spannung, und es ist ein intimer Akt des Malens",[3] so die Künstlerin. Die Farborgien ihrer Gemälde strahlen eine kraftvolle und zugleich zarte Sinnlichkeit aus; kleinteilige Formen fügen sich zu größeren dynamischen Bewegungsmustern zusammen – nicht so sehr berechnete Formationen, sondern vielmehr Kräfte. Die Arbeiten spiegeln auch das Interesse der Künstlerin an der Farbmaterialität, ihrer unterschiedlichen Dichte, ihren Eigenschaften und Artikulationsmöglichkeiten, ihrer nicht-illusionistischen Rauheit, ihrer mit Feminität assozi-

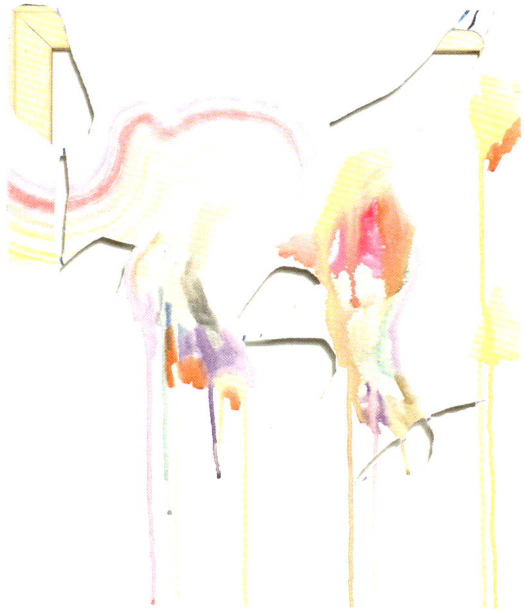

Cut-Out, watercolour/marker on linen, 60 × 50 cm, 2019

1 Georgia O'Keeffe, in: David W. Galenson, *Conceptual Revolutions in Twentieth-Century Art*, Cambridge 2009, S. 97, Übers. d. Autorin.

2 Lucio Fontana, in: Carla Lonzi, *Autoritratto. Accardi, Alviani, Castellani, Consagra, Fabro, Fontana, Kounellis, Nigro, Paolini, Pascali, Rotella, Scarpitta, Turcato, Twombly*, Bari 1969, S. 169–171, Übers. d. Autorin.

3 Patricia Reinhart im Gespräch im November 2021.

ierten Sensibilität. Patricia Reinhart nutzt das ganze Farbspektrum, dem Prinzipien der Optik und Physik inhärent sind, und verwandelt es in einen malerischen Erfahrungsraum, in dem wir träumen dürfen.

Abstrakte Farb-Form-Strukturen können als ausdehnbarer innerer Raum und als Vorstellung vom kosmischen Raum des Weltalls interpretiert werden: Sie lassen sich unendlich fortsetzen, da die Begrenzung durch das Gegenständliche fehlt. Eine derartige „Vermessung der Welt", wie Patricia Reinhart eine Bildserie (*NM*, 2020–2022) genannt hat, visualisiert sich abstrakt als Ausdruck von Vorstellungskraft. Raumtiefe entsteht durch Schichten von Hell-Dunkel-Kontrasten, die sich durch ein gestaffeltes Neben- und Übereinander von zarten und kräftigen Farben, das heißt von dünnerem oder dickerem Farbauftrag, in unterschiedlichen Formationen bilden. Gezeichnete Elemente durchqueren die polymorphen Farbstrukturen und erinnern an Zirkel, diagrammatische Fragmente oder räumliche Markierungen. Brodelnde Himmel, Feuerwerke, Explosionen, Unwetter oder sich in ständiger Veränderung und Bewegung befindende Energien als Visualisierungen innerer Zustände deuten darauf hin, dass die Unendlichkeit des Raumes eher innerlich erfahren werden kann als durch eine objektive Ansicht. Zwar erahnen wir bei einem Blick auf den Horizont am Meer, in den klaren Nachthimmel oder bei einer Flugreise über den Wolken einen unendlichen Raum. Nachdem die Unendlichkeit aber keinen Gesamtüberblick zulässt, können wir diesen Raum visuell nur als Fragment oder symbolhaft erfassen. Eine gemalte Unendlichkeit spannt auf der Leinwand einen symbolischen Raum mit einer imaginären Ausdehnung auf. Ein kulturelles Sinnbild für einen auf diese Weise doppelt gedachten materiellen und mentalen, psychischen oder spirituellen Raum ist das himmlische Paradies, das als Garten irdisch verortet wird. Diesem widmet sich Patricia Reinhart mit der Serie *Paradise I–III* (2018–2020).

Wie es die Beispiele bedeutender Künstler:innen des 20. Jahrhunderts – von Hilma af Klint über Piet Mondrian und Kasimir Malewitsch bis Lee Krasner – zeigen, ist die Geschichte der abstrakten Malerei davon durchzogen, nichtgegenständliche Kompositionen als Darstellung geistig-spiritueller Dimensionen zu verstehen. Patricia Reinharts mehrteilige Serien wie *Coïncidences* (2021/22) oder *Patience* (2015/16) sind als konzeptuelle Analogie zwischen abstrakten Formen und abstrakten Konzepten von Raum, Zeit und Begegnung angelegt. Insbesondere die Farbe stellt durch ihre verdichteten stofflichen Eigenschaften enge Beziehungen zwischen materiellen und nicht-materiellen Welten her. Sie kann Ausgangspunkt für Betrachtungen auf physikalischer, neurologischer oder psychologischer Ebene sein, die innere und äußere Räume gleichermaßen berühren. Sie kann auf kultureller Ebene in den Bereich der Mystik führen oder auf wissenschaftlicher in die Quantenphysik. Als subjektiver Ausdruck nähert sich die Malerei von Patricia Reinhart den der Welt eingeschriebenen Gesetzmäßigkeiten an und verortet darin das eigene Selbst.

Synne Genzmer arbeitet als freie Kuratorin und Autorin. Studium der Kunstgeschichte an der Universität Wien. 2007–2012 im kuratorischen Team der Kunsthalle Wien. 2013/14 Publikationsmanagement bei der Generali Foundation, Wien.

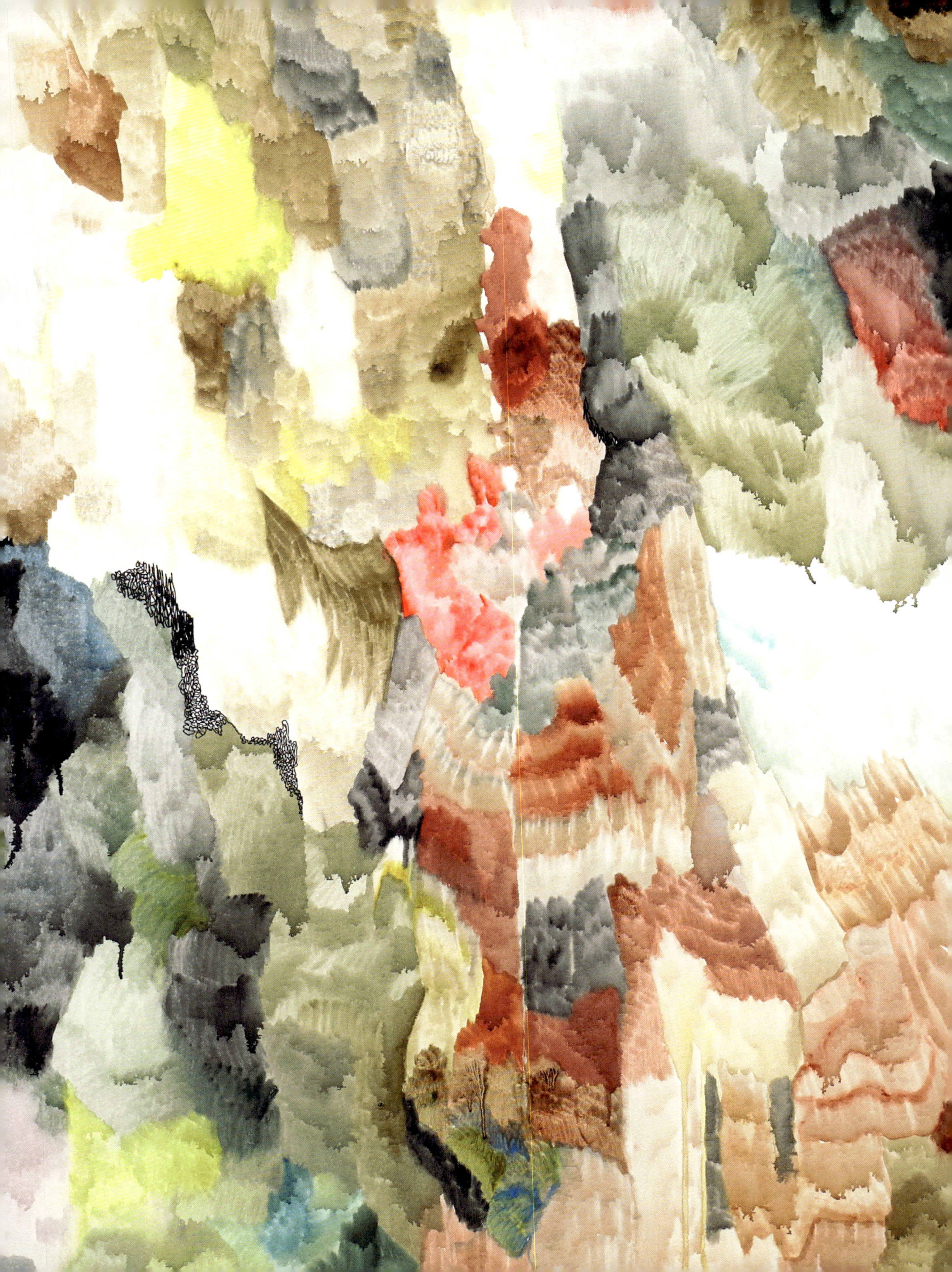

Kaléidoscope et cosmos Des abstractions en peinture

Synne Genzmer

... choisir une ligne d'action bien précise et s'y tenir.[1] —Georgia O'Keeffe

La découverte du cosmos est une nouvelle dimension. [...] La découverte du cosmos par Einstein est une dimension infinie, sans fin. Nous avons donc ici : le premier plan, le centre et l'arrière-plan. [...] Pour continuer, que dois-je faire ? [...] Je fais des trous, l'infini passe à travers eux, la lumière passe à travers eux, pas besoin de peindre.[2] —Lucio Fontana

Perforer ou abîmer volontairement la toile est devenu au XXe siècle un moyen d'expression et un geste symbolique. Cela a élevé le violent et le destructeur au rang d'éléments esthétiques, mais a aussi été une avancée vers de nouvelles dimensions, soulignant à la fois le réel et le métaphorique de la peinture : Niki de Saint-Phalle tirait sur ses reliefs dans un acte d'émancipation, Joan Miró présentait ses *Burnt Canvases* pour protester contre l'oppression politique et la réduction de l'art à une marchandise destinée à une société élitiste. Enfin, avec son *Concetto spaziale*, Lucio Fontana voulait élargir la surface de la toile et l'ouvrir sur l'espace infini.

Ces artistes travaillaient tous, à leur façon, avec une surface négative, littéralement un espace vide, qui – sous forme de trous, de perforations, de coupes ou de surfaces découpées – acquiert une force créatrice. Un espace qui n'est pas seulement représenté, mais qui existe réellement. Dans ses *Cut-Outs*, Patricia Reinhart utilise la découpe comme un outil précis qui ne détruit pas les formes peintes de ses images, mais les imite. Elle découpe ou évide ses compositions de façon contrôlée et précise, se servant du couteau comme d'un scalpel correctif. La peinture se fait alors sculpture, et sa fragilité en est perturbée. L'artiste sculpte la toile en y extrayant, comme d'un corps, les parties qui doivent nécessairement être enlevées pour que le tableau fonctionne. Apparaissent des vues et perspectives vers un arrière, vers le mur derrière la toile ou vers une autre pièce. Comme des « sandwich paintings », ce sont des couches qui, peinture devant la peinture, doublent l'espace peint. De nombreux *Cut-Outs* laissent visibles les châssis, sur lesquels seules d'étroites bandes de toiles sont tendues. Les *Cut-Outs* jettent des ombres sur les murs, ils provoquent sous nos yeux des effets physiques, révélant l'illusion de la peinture, d'une surface uniforme brisée par l'espace réel.

Dans ses premières années, Patricia Reinhart utilisait le medium de la peinture pour des esquisses et des dessins préparatoires figuratifs, en parallèle à ses films muets, dans lesquels elle abordait le rôle de la femme selon divers cadres historico-culturels et d'après des modèles littéraires (*Untitled*, 2007). Cette interaction caractérise également certains de ses pastels à l'huile de 2012 et 2013, qui évoquent le thème du jardin, lorsque la surface s'emplit de formes végétales et que la nature se fait ornement. Dans l'œuvre *Untitled* (2014), on distingue une affinité avec les formes végétales de Matisse, présentes en peinture puis en découpages dans l'œuvre du peintre moderniste, qui, sous forme de papier découpé, ont migré de la toile vers les murs mêmes de son atelier. Considérer la peinture comme un espace dont les structures abstraites dérivent d'un jardin nous conduit tout droit aux *Nymphéas* de Monet. En tant qu'installation permanente au Musée de l'Orangerie à Paris, la toile épouse quasiment les murs ovales, se superpose à l'espace de présentation, en devient indiscernable. Les surfaces de taches de couleurs qui, à distance, deviennent sur nos rétines un tapis de nénuphars, préfigurent le all-over abstrait d'un Jackson Pollock. Via cette installation, le jardin attiré à l'intérieur fait se confondre le dedans et le dehors, et transforme la galerie en un paysage illusionniste qui se déploie le long des murs. Un jardin, c'est aussi le décor du film de Patricia Reinhart *Anoir and the Woman in the Garden* (2015–2017), dans lequel une protagoniste vêtue de blanc se meut au milieu de plantes exotiques luxuriantes. Le bassin au centre, dans lequel se reflètent la nature et le ciel, semble être le miroir filmique de sa peinture abstraite

Detail *Patience XIV – Attitude / Das weibliche Rückgrat*, watercolour/marker on linen, 170 × 150 cm, 2016

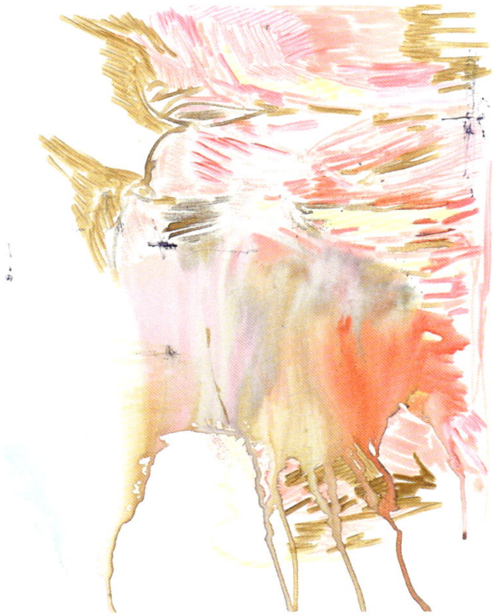

If days are dogs, watercolour/marker on linen, 50 × 40 cm, 2018

et de sa vibration paysagère. Le jardin, emblème d'un espace féminin à soi, a une forte signification symbolique qui souligne la posture de l'artiste et sa vive conscience d'être *une* peintre et d'occuper de manière contemporaine et avec verve, en tant que femme, un rôle qui fut si longtemps masculin.

Le début d'un séjour parisien de plusieurs années coïncida avec la découverte de l'aquarelle, qui a remplacé l'intense et expressionniste peinture sur toile à l'huile imprégnée de térébenthine. Avec une technique de peinture bien particulière, en glacis, qui soulignait et utilisait l'aspect aqueux, liquide et fluide des couleurs, apparurent de nouvelles dimensions picturales dans les thèmes et les structures, et avec elles un glissement vers l'abstraction. Alors que Patricia Reinhart avait précédemment travaillé le pastel à l'huile, générant des formes oscillantes entre figuratif et abstraction, elle se libère des structures figuratives avec l'aquarelle. Dans ses nombreuses peintures, une affinité avec la narration ou la représentation est encore perceptible à travers les formes abstraites. Néanmoins, ses œuvres témoignent moins d'un intérêt pour la saisie figurative et limitée de phénomènes que pour leur représentation comme des effets de forces et d'énergies. Un tourbillon de couleurs et de formes énergiques peut ainsi illustrer une tempête en lieu et place de la restitution du phénomène naturel tel qu'on peut l'observer.

Patricia Reinhart n'emploie pas l'aquarelle de façon conventionnelle. Sa technique particulière intègre consciemment les propriétés fluides de l'aquarelle, de l'écoulement, du ruissellement de la couleur, de l'étalement en surface, dans les compositions créées intuitivement et sans dessin préalable. Elle les utilise pour certaines formations esthétiques directement sur toile blanche. Cette technique semble également adaptée à la représentativité de processus et espaces internes, inconscients et émotionnels. Des œuvres comme *XXV – W VI (Sleep 5/3)* (2021) ou *Cut-Out / Lucid Dream* (2018) trahissent une inspiration psychanalytique. Une visualisation de structures psychiques n'est pas un programme artistique, mais participe d'une recherche autoréférencée vers le vrai, l'authentique et la métaphysique, ainsi que d'une forme de méditation qui se caractérise par son authenticité : « Le trait est vrai, il a sa propre tension, et c'est un acte intime de peinture »,[3] selon l'artiste. Les orgies de couleurs de ses peintures dégagent une sensualité à la fois forte et tendre, qui assemble des formes minuscules en de plus grands motifs de mouvements dynamiques. Ce sont plutôt des forces que des formations calculées. Elles reflètent l'intérêt de l'artiste pour la matérialité de cette couleur, ses variations de densité, ses propriétés et ses possibilités d'articulation, sa crudité naturelle, sa sensibilité associée à la féminité. Patricia Reinhart se sert de tout le spectre coloré, aux inhérents principes optiques et physiques, et transforme son tableau en un espace d'expérience picturale, dans lequel nous sommes encouragés à rêver.

Les structures abstraites de couleurs et de formes peuvent aussi être interprétées comme un espace intérieur extensible et comme la représentation d'un espace cosmique qui ouvre vers une infinie immensité. Leurs découpes respectives peuvent être prolongées à l'infini, car elles ne sont pas limitées par la représentativité. Un tel « arpentage du monde », selon l'intitulé donné par Patricia Reinhart à une série de tableaux (*NM*, 2020–2022), se visualise de manière

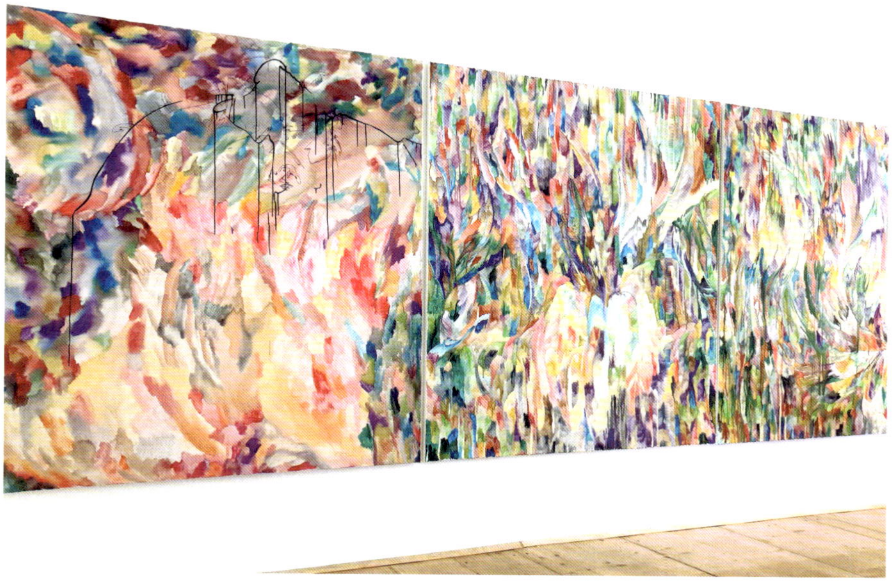

Studio view Vienna / Atelieransicht Wien / Vue d'atelier Vienne, 2021

abstraite comme une expression de l'imagination. La profondeur de l'espace est créée par des couches de contrastes clair-obscur formés par juxtaposition et superposition échelonnée de couleurs tendres et vives, c'est-à-dire par application de peinture plus ou moins fine ou épaisse, dans différentes combinaisons. Des éléments dessinés traversent les structures chromatiques polymorphes et évoquent des compas, des fragments diagrammatiques ou des repères spatiaux. Ciels bouillonnants, feux d'artifices, explosions, tempêtes ou énergies en perpétuelle évolution : autant de visualisations d'états intérieurs qui indiquent que l'infinité de l'espace peut être expérimentée intérieurement plutôt que par une vue objective. Certes, nous ressentons l'infinité de l'espace par un regard vers l'horizon marin, un ciel nocturne dégagé ou un vol au-dessus des nuages. Comme il est impossible d'avoir une vue d'ensemble de l'infini, nous ne pouvons appréhender visuellement cet espace que sous forme de fragments ou de symboles. Un infini peint ouvre sur la toile un espace symbolique dont l'extension est laissée à l'imagination. Le paradis céleste, qui se manifeste sur la terre comme un jardin, est un symbole culturel pour un espace ainsi doublement pensé comme étant matériel et mental, psychique et spirituel. C'est à ce jardin que Patricia Reinhart dédie sa série *Paradise I–III* (2018–2020).

Comme le montrent les exemples d'artistes importants du XXe siècle – de Hilma af Klint, Piet Mondrian et Kasimir Malevitch à Lee Krasner – l'histoire de la peinture abstraite est traversée par la compréhension de compositions non-figuratives comme représentation de dimensions spirituelles et intellectuelles. Les séries en plusieurs parties de Patricia Reinhart, comme *Coïncidences* (2021/2022) ou *Patience* (2015/2016), tracent des analogies conceptuelles entre les formes et concepts abstraits d'espace, de temps et de rencontre. La couleur, en particulier, établit des relations étroites entre mondes matériels et immatériels dont les propriétés sont condensées en matérialité. La couleur peut être le point de départ d'une réflexion sur le plan physique, neurologique ou psychologique, qui touche autant les espaces intérieurs qu'extérieurs. Au niveau culturel, elle peut conduire à la mystique ; au niveau scientifique, à la physique quantique. En tant qu'expression subjective, la peinture de Patricia Reinhart se rapproche des principes qui gouvernent le monde et situe l'être même en leur sein.

Synne Genzmer est curatrice et autrice indépendante. Études d'histoire de l'art à l'Université de Vienne. 2007–2012 membre de l'équipe curatoriale de la Kunsthalle Wien. 2013/2014 directrice des publications, Generali Foundation, Vienne.

1 Georgia O'Keeffe, dans : David W. Galenson, *Conceptual Revolutions in Twentieth-Century Art*, Cambridge 2009, p. 97, traduction par l'autrice.

2 Lucio Fontana, dans : Carla Lonzi, *Autoritratto. Accardi, Alviani, Castellani, Consagra, Fabro, Fontana, Kounellis, Nigro, Paolini, Pascali, Rotella, Scarpitta, Turcato, Twombly*, Bari 1969, p. 169–171, traduction par l'autrice.

3 Entretien avec Patricia Reinhart, novembre 2021.

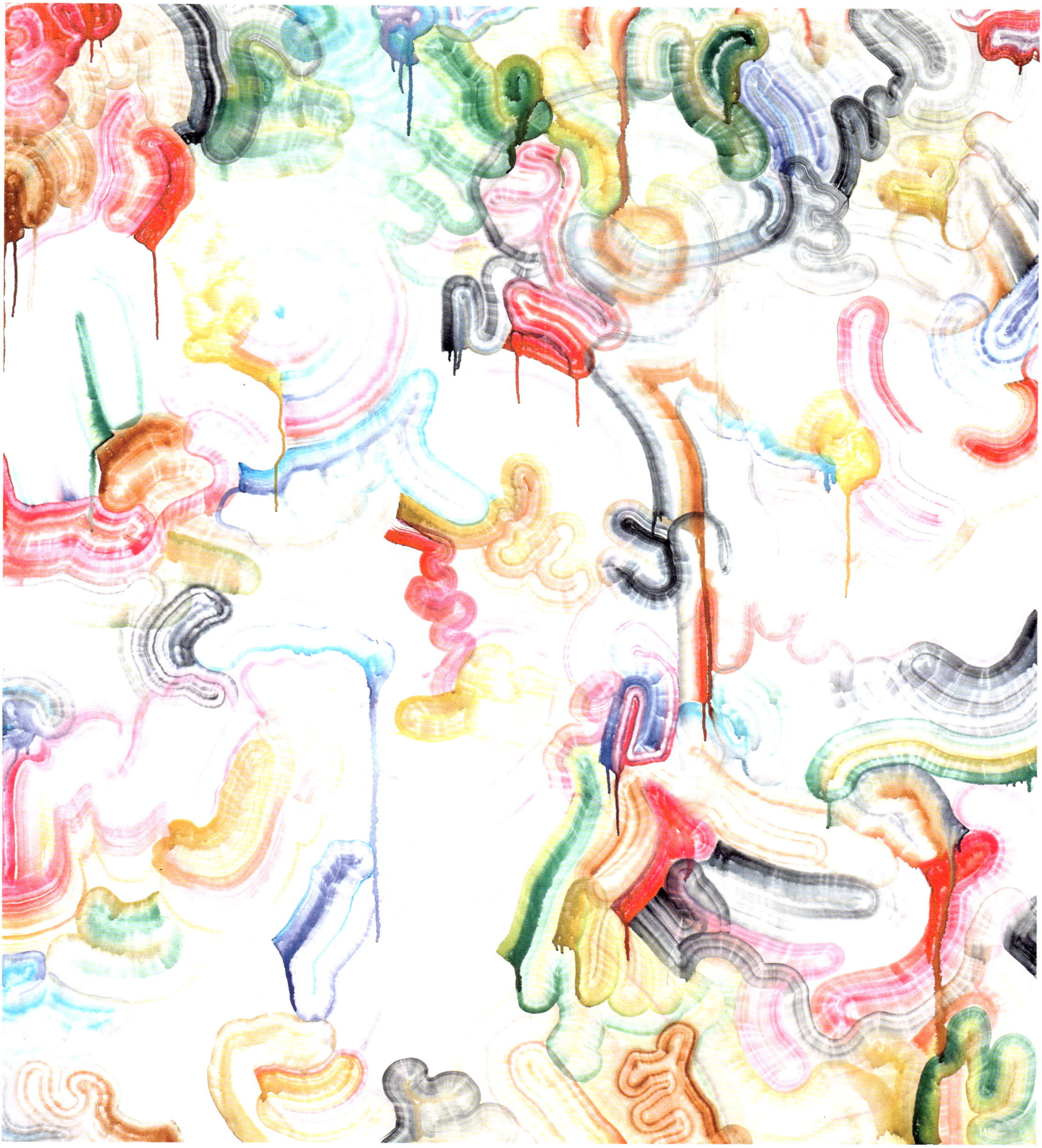

Untitled, watercolour/marker on linen, 170 × 150 cm, 2019

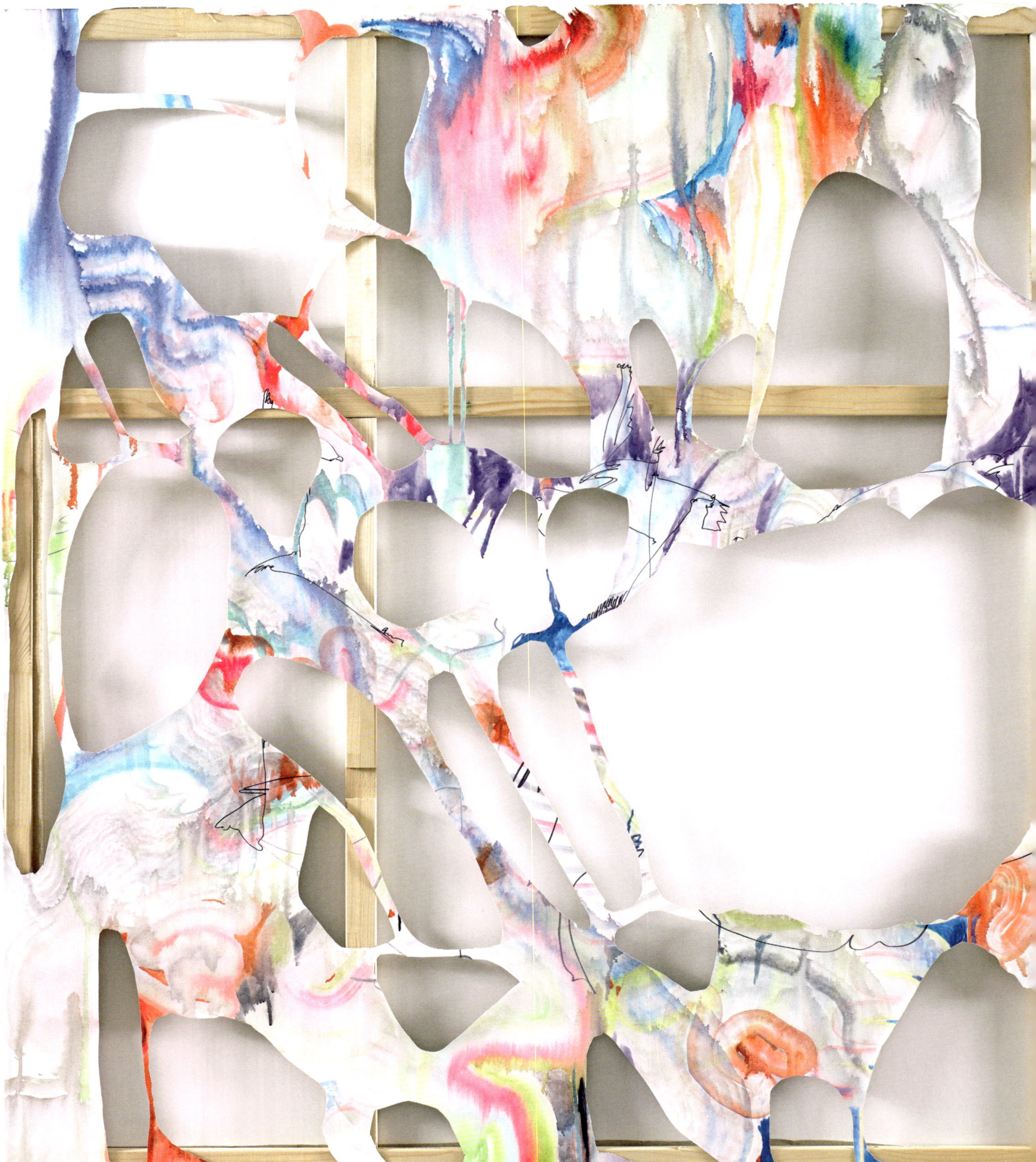

Cut-Out, watercolour/marker on linen, 170 × 150 cm, 2019

Untitled (Sleep 5/2), watercolour/marker on linen, 170 × 150 cm, 2019

Untitled (Sleep 5/1), watercolour/marker on linen, 170 × 150 cm, 2019

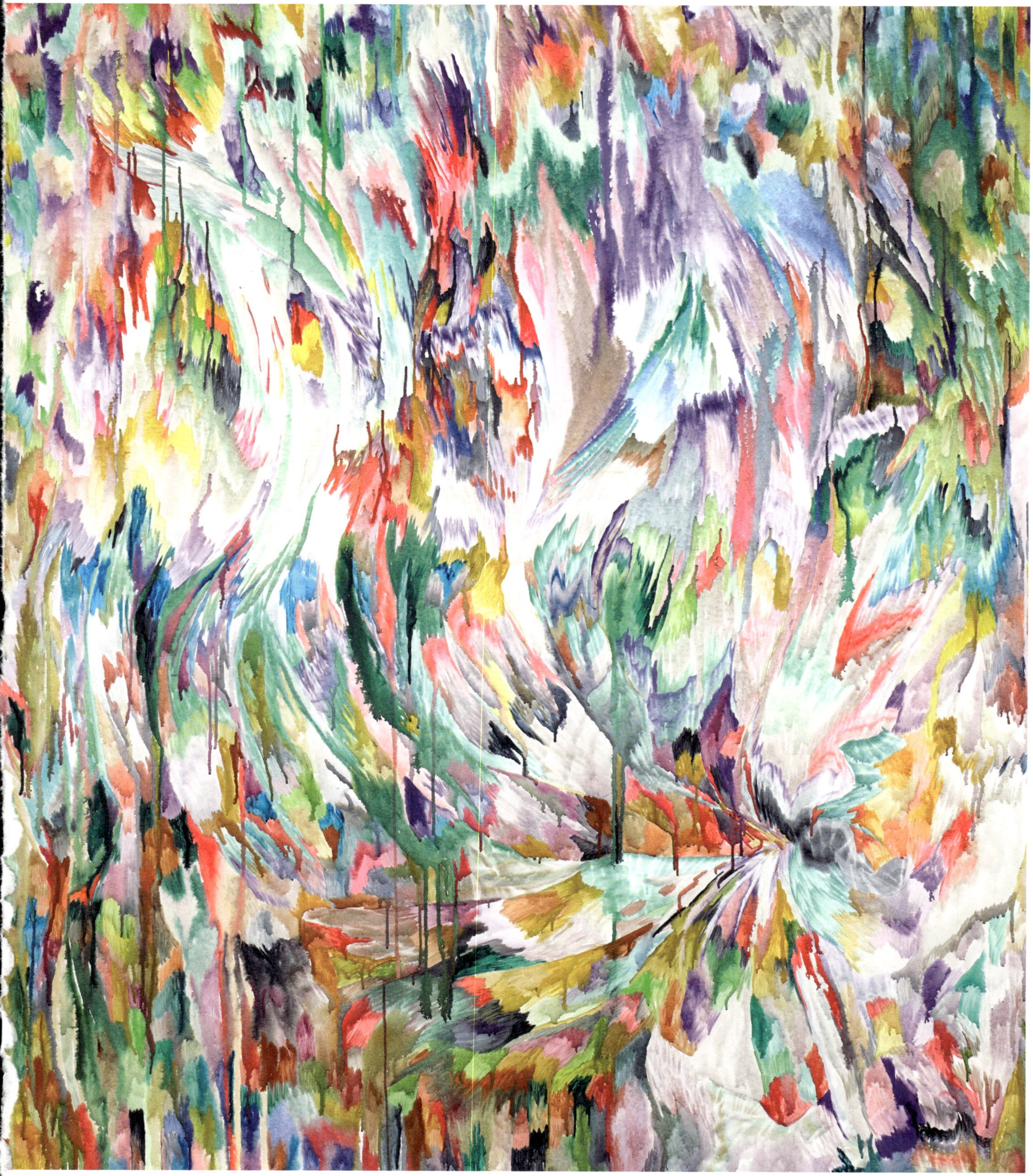

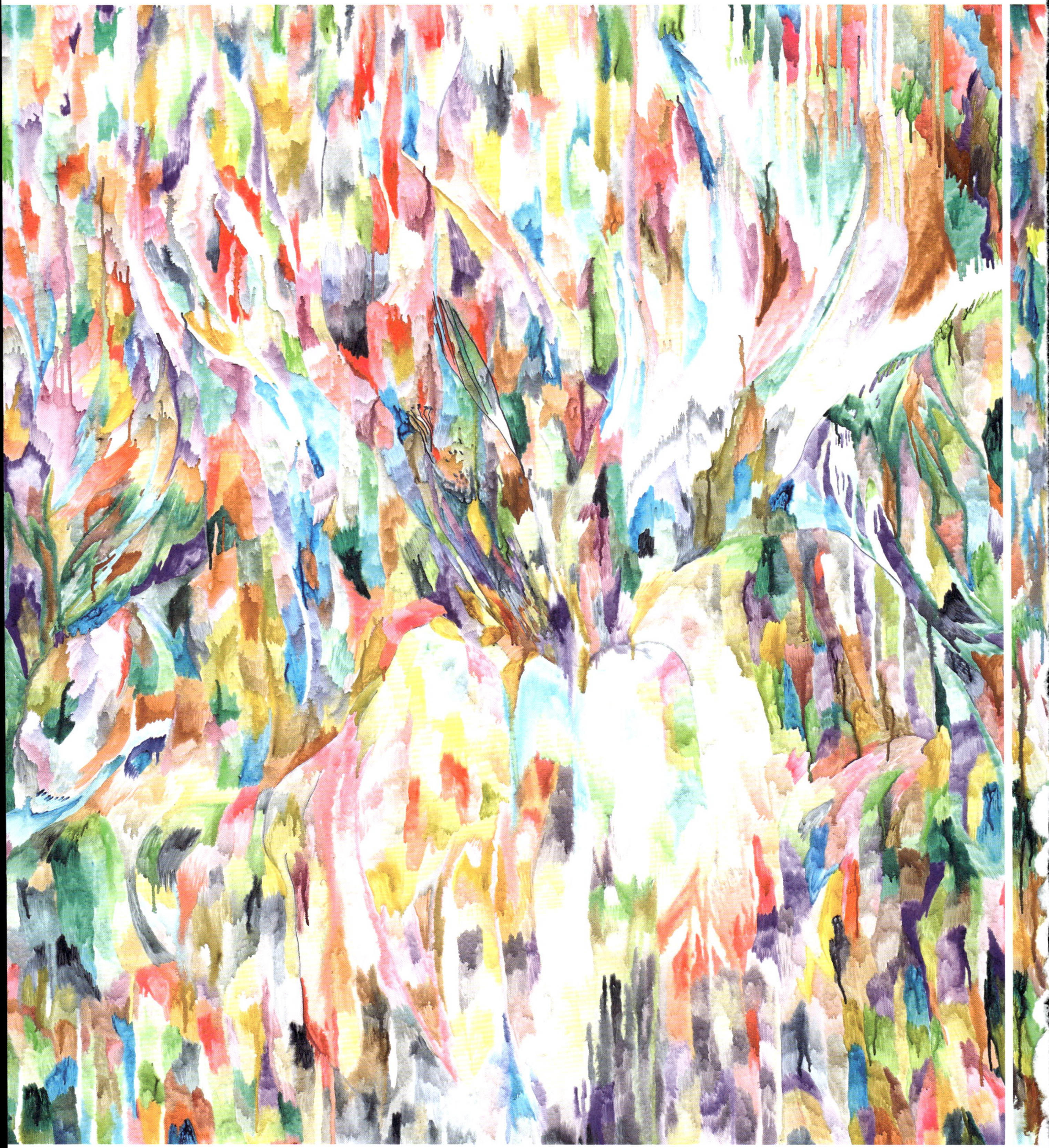

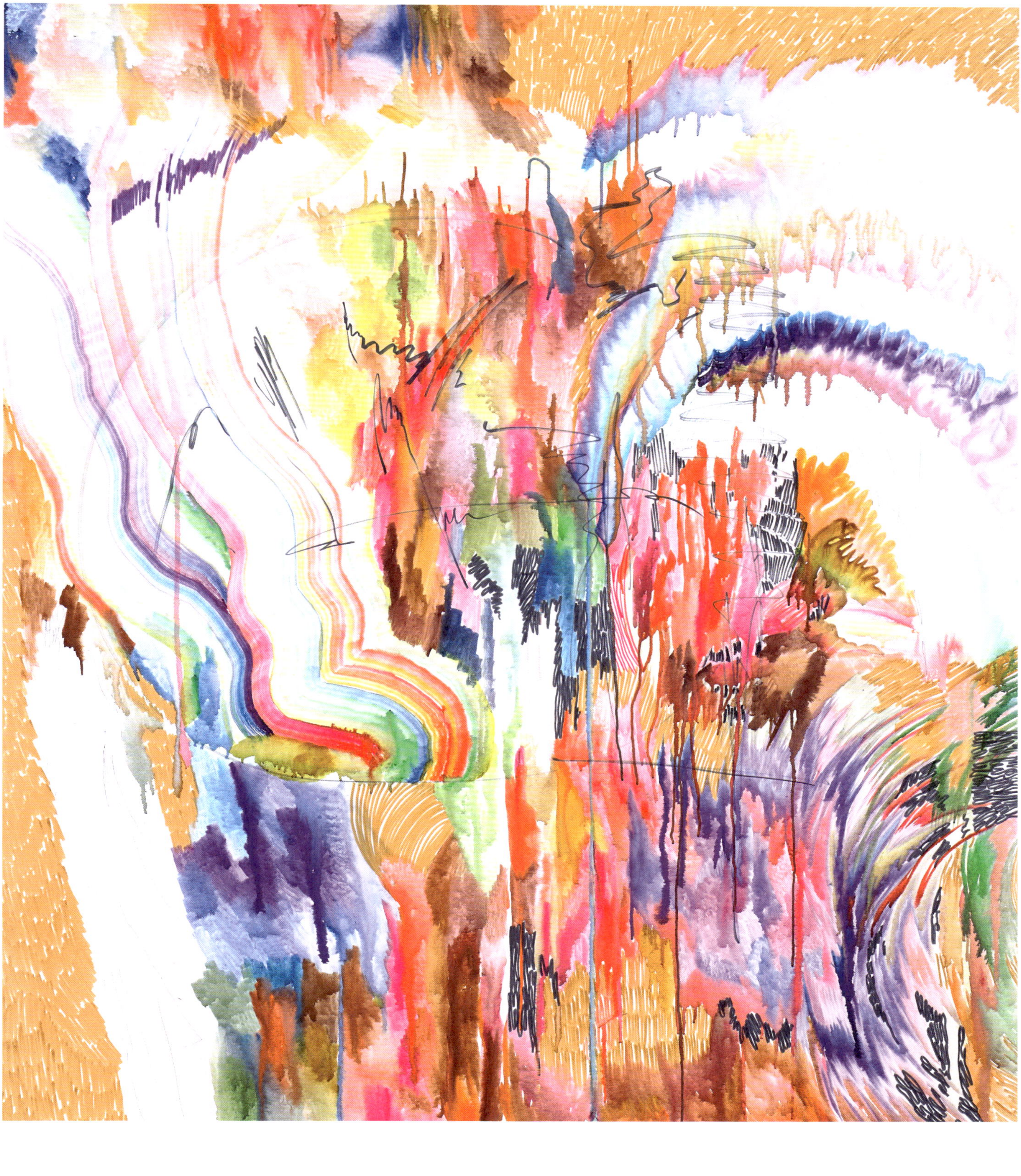

IX – VI / Paradise III (NM), watercolour/marker on linen, 170 × 150 cm, 2020

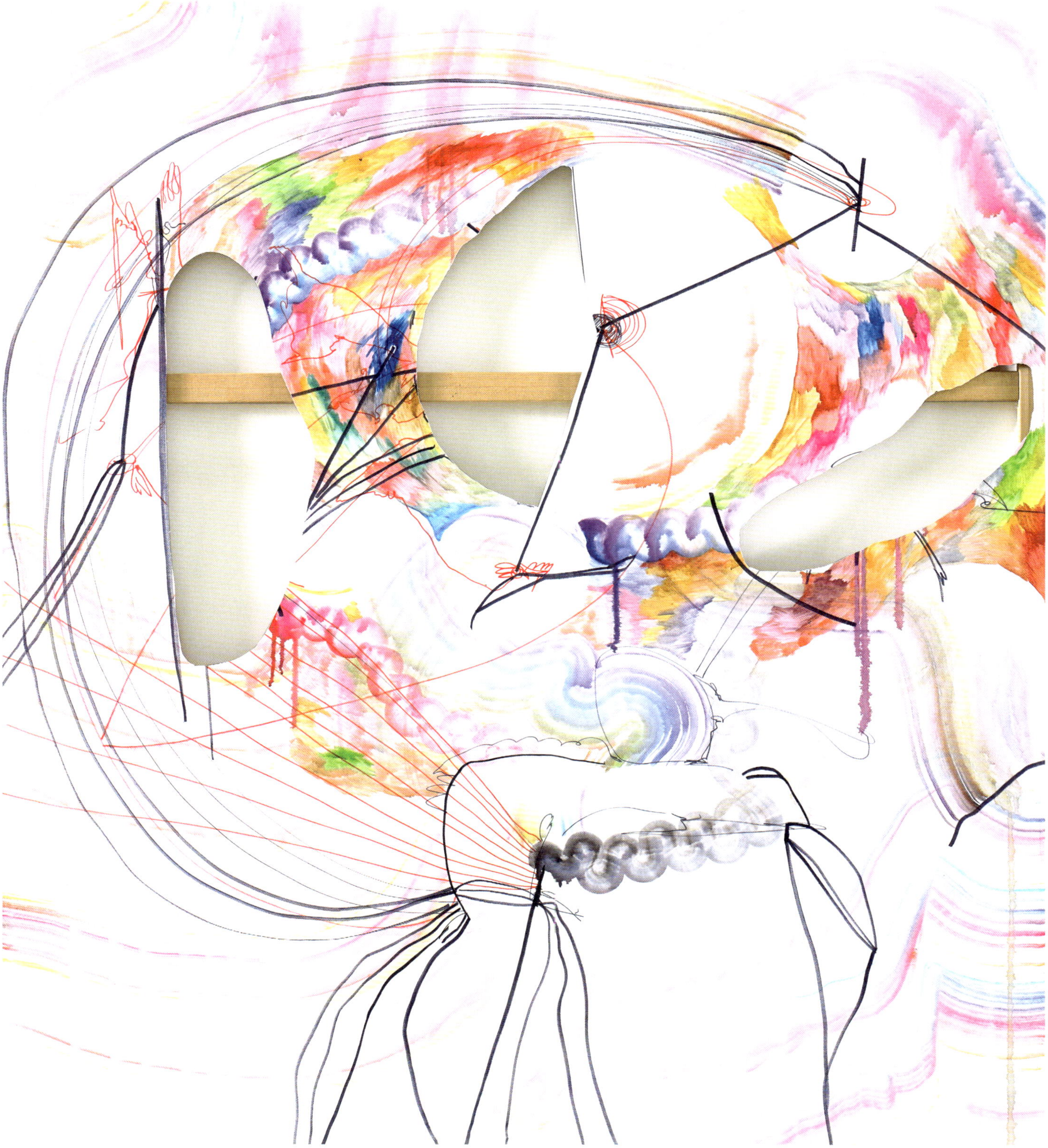

V – Vermessung I (NM), watercolour/marker on linen, 170 × 150 cm, 2020

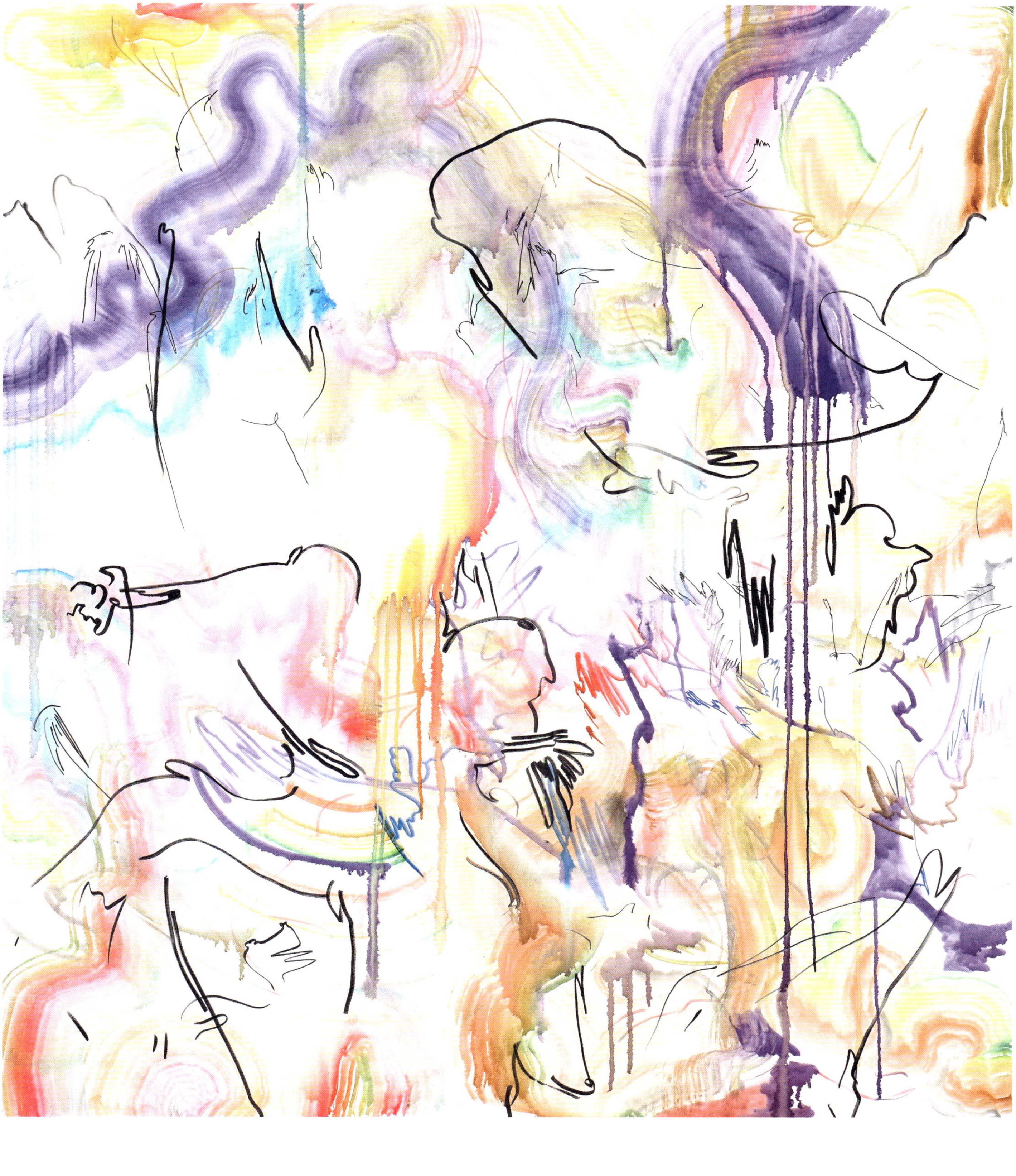

Untitled (Girl with Dogs), watercolour/marker on linen, 170 × 150 cm, 2019

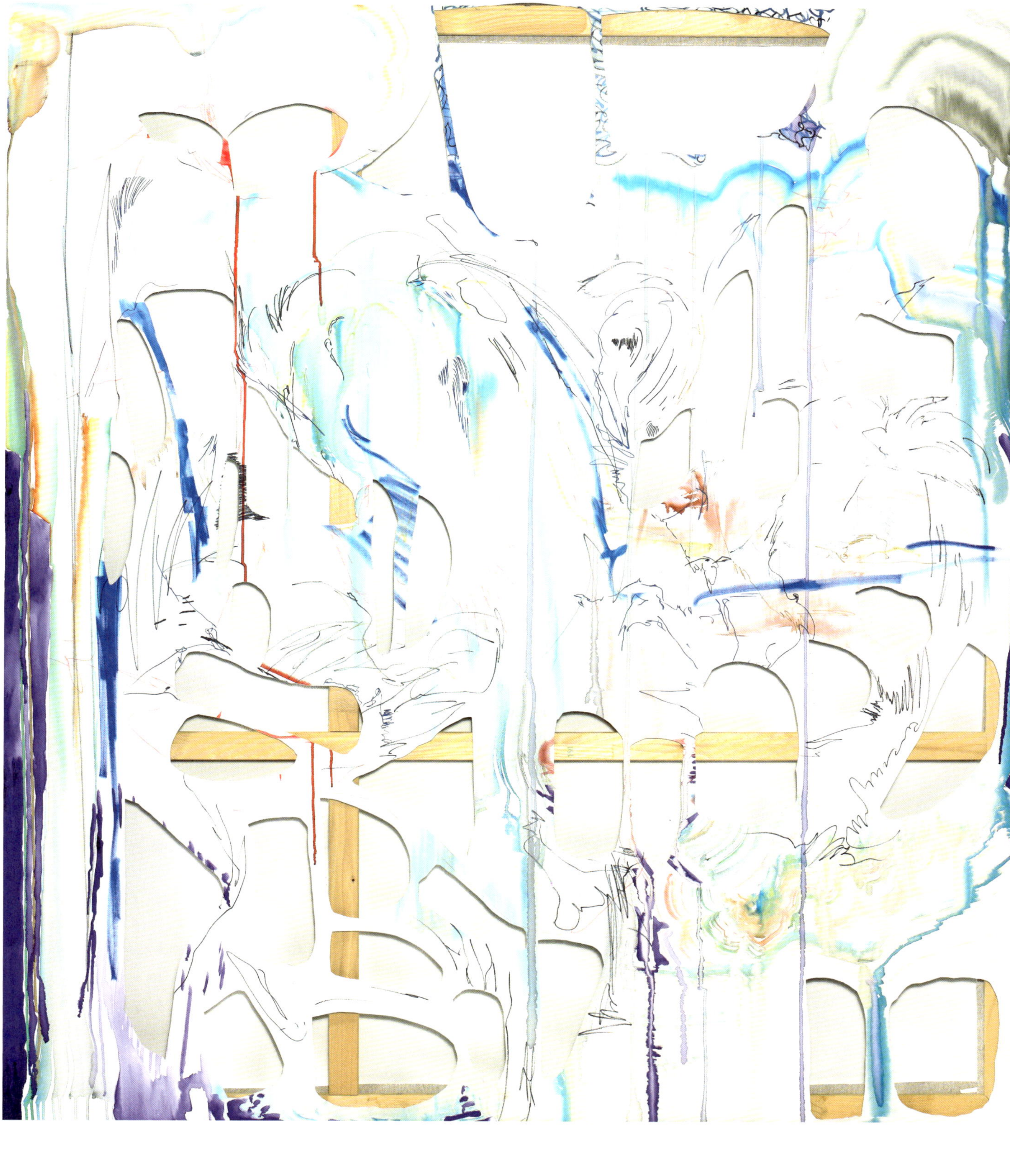

Cut-Out / Lucid Dream, watercolour/marker on linen, 170 × 150 cm, 2018

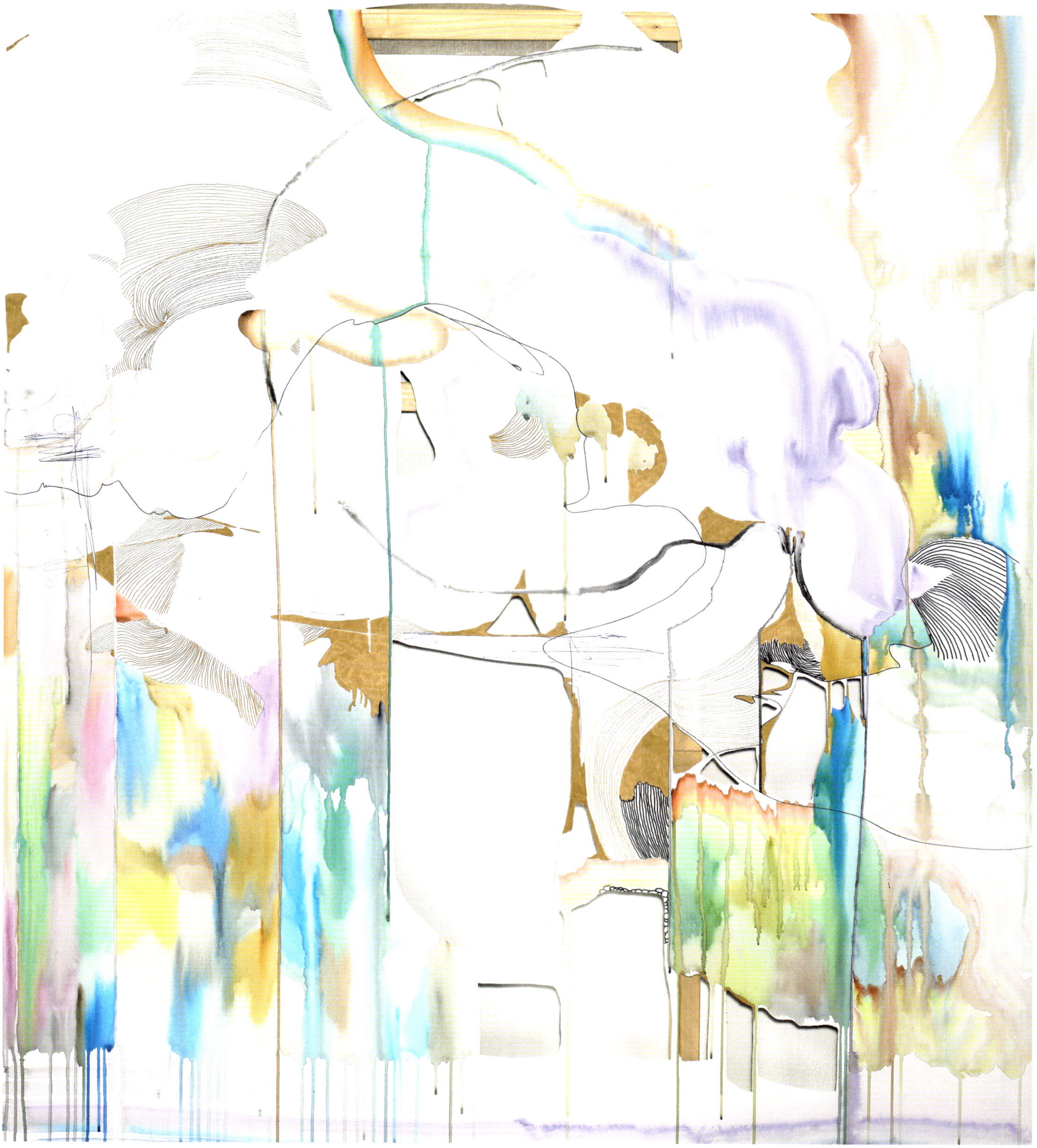

Cut-Out (Sentimental Bird), watercolour/marker on linen, 170 × 150 cm, 2018

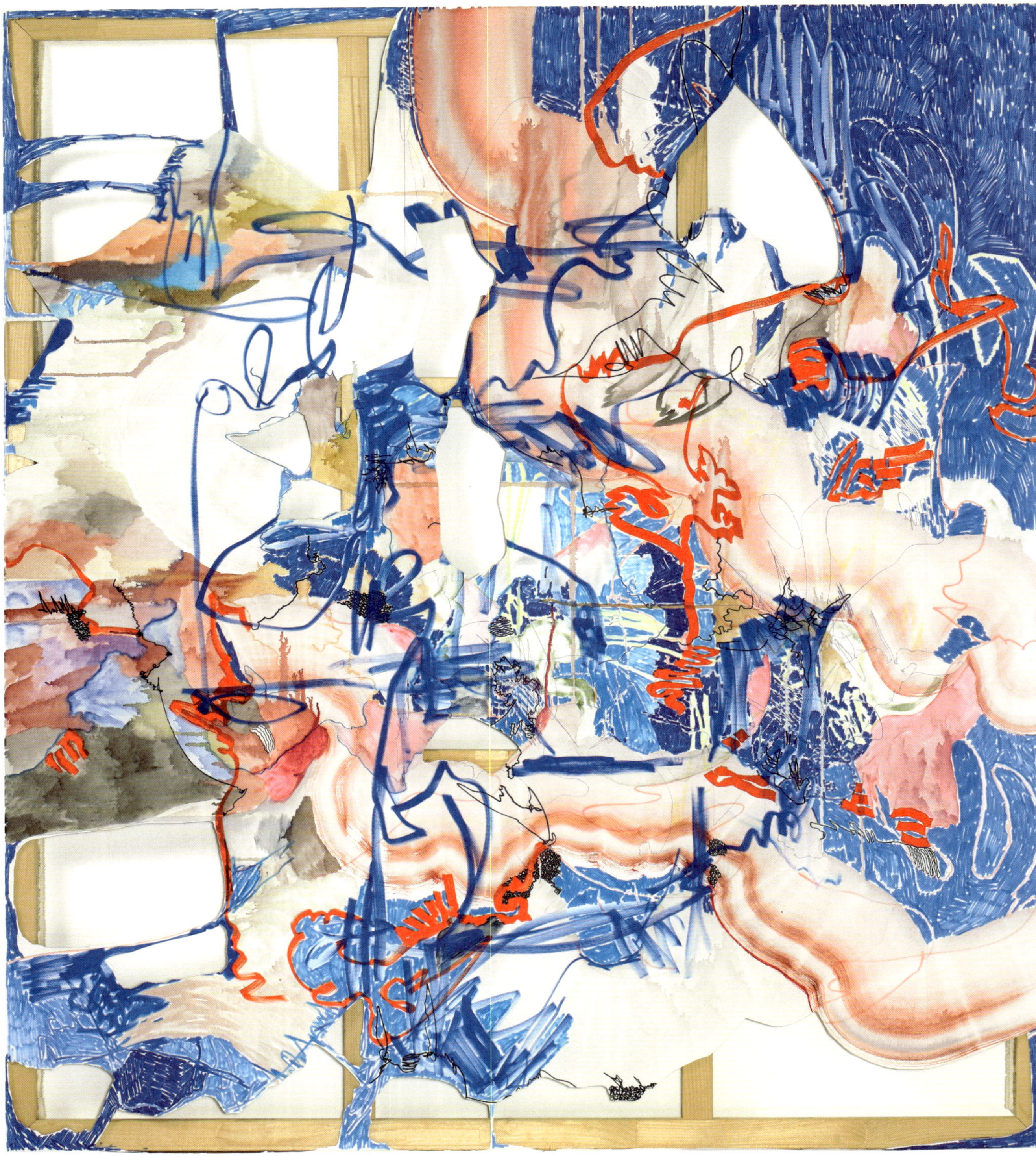

Cut-Out / Ein Kräftemessen von Farbe und Linie, watercolour/acryl/marker on linen, 170 × 150 cm, 2017

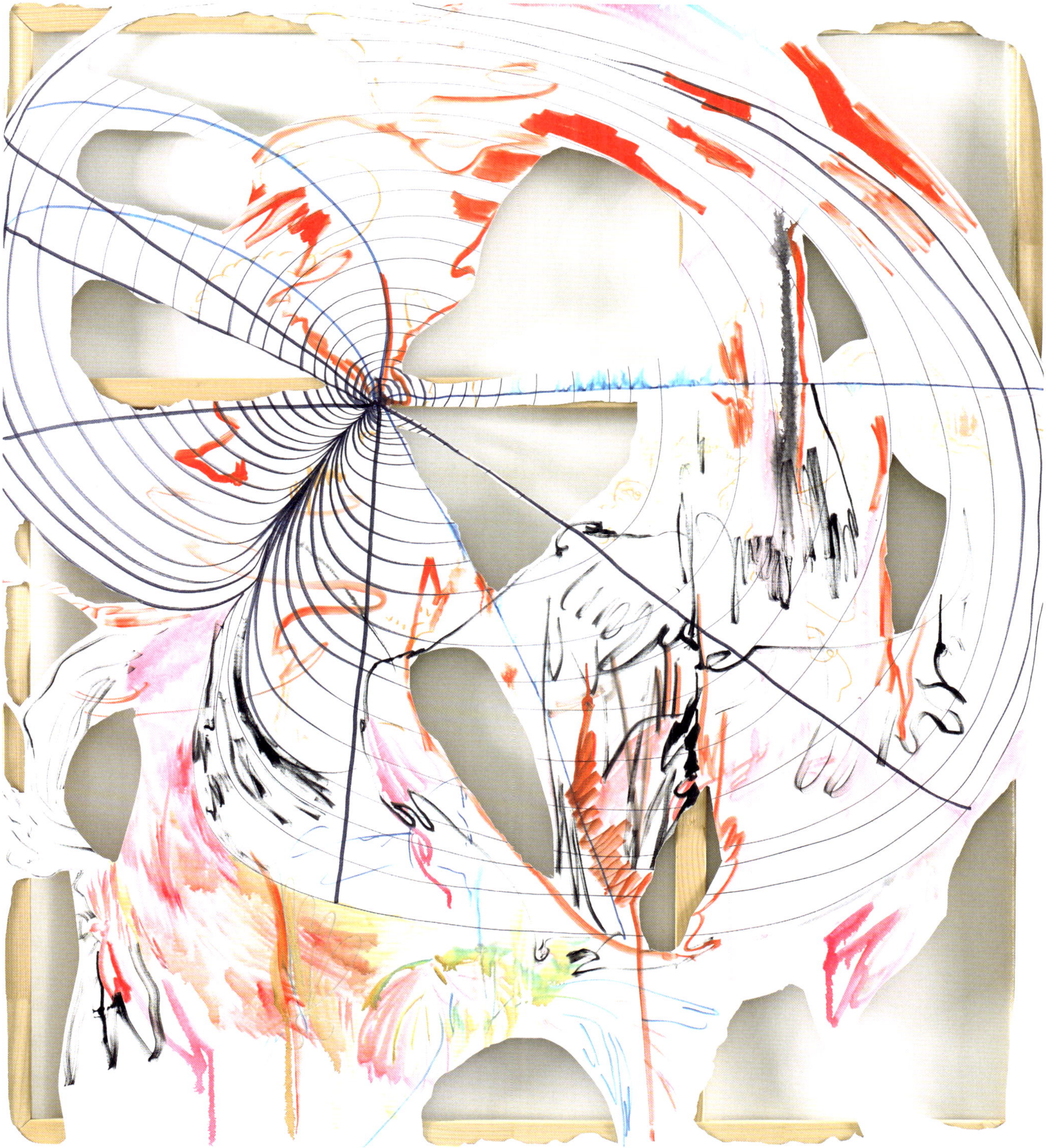

Cut-Out, watercolour/marker on linen, 170 × 150 cm, 2019

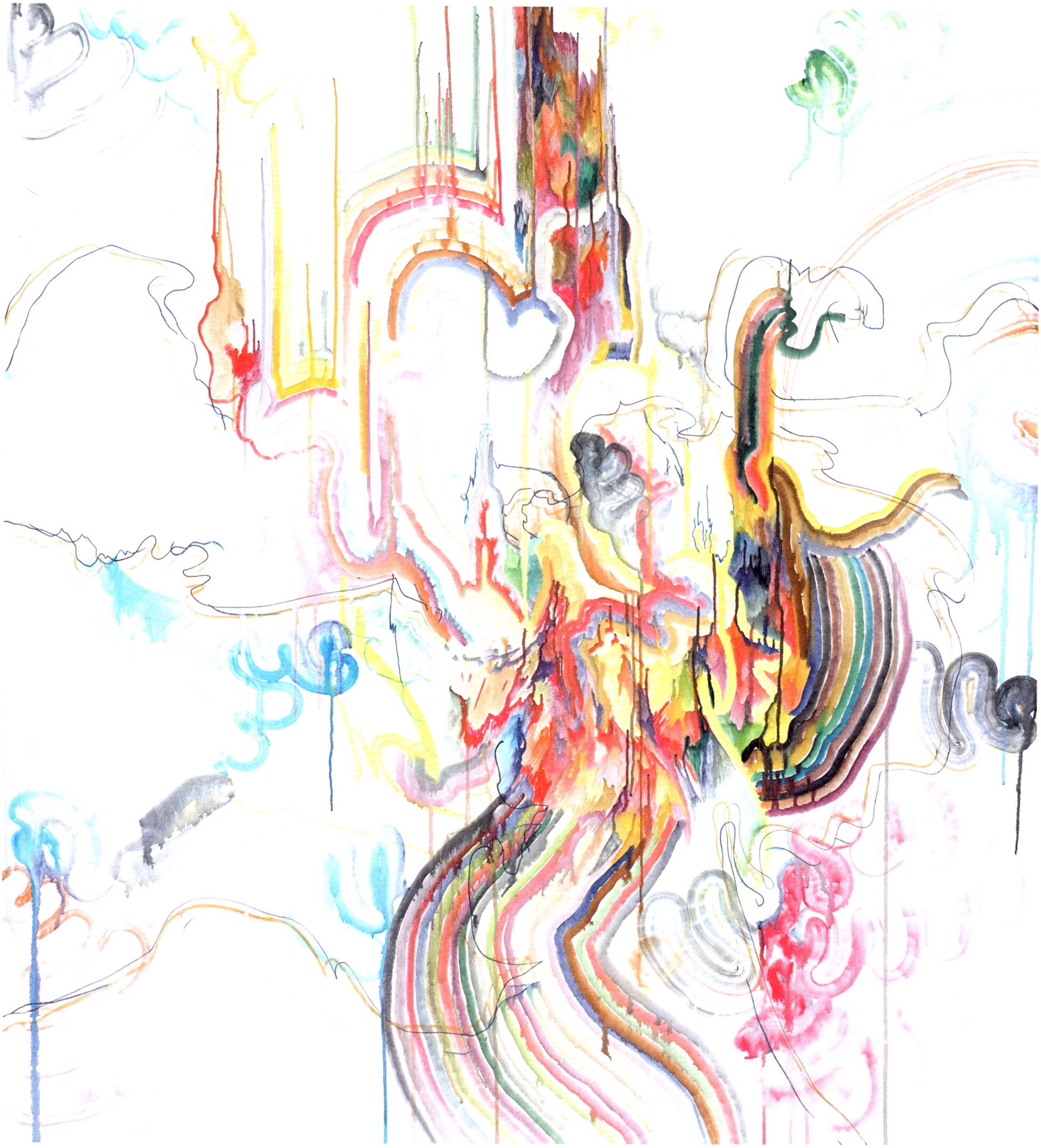

Untitled (The Napping Roamer), watercolour/marker on linen, 170 × 150 cm, 2019

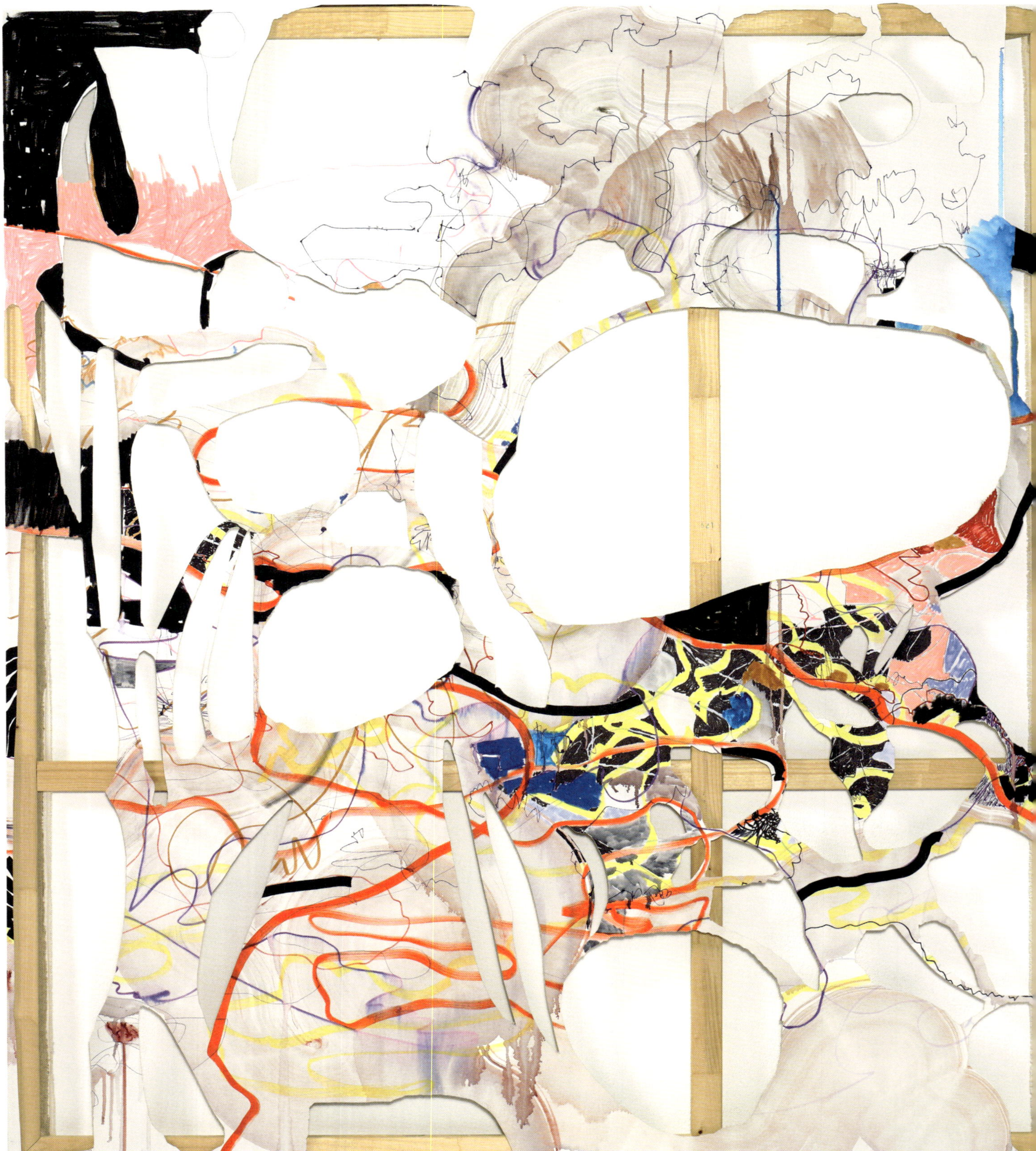

Cut-Out, watercolour/acryl/marker on linen, 170 × 150 cm, 2017

Cut-Out / Sundogs, watercolour/acryl/marker on linen, 170 × 150 cm, 2018

Untitled (Milky Way), watercolour/acryl/marker on linen, 170 × 150 cm, 2018

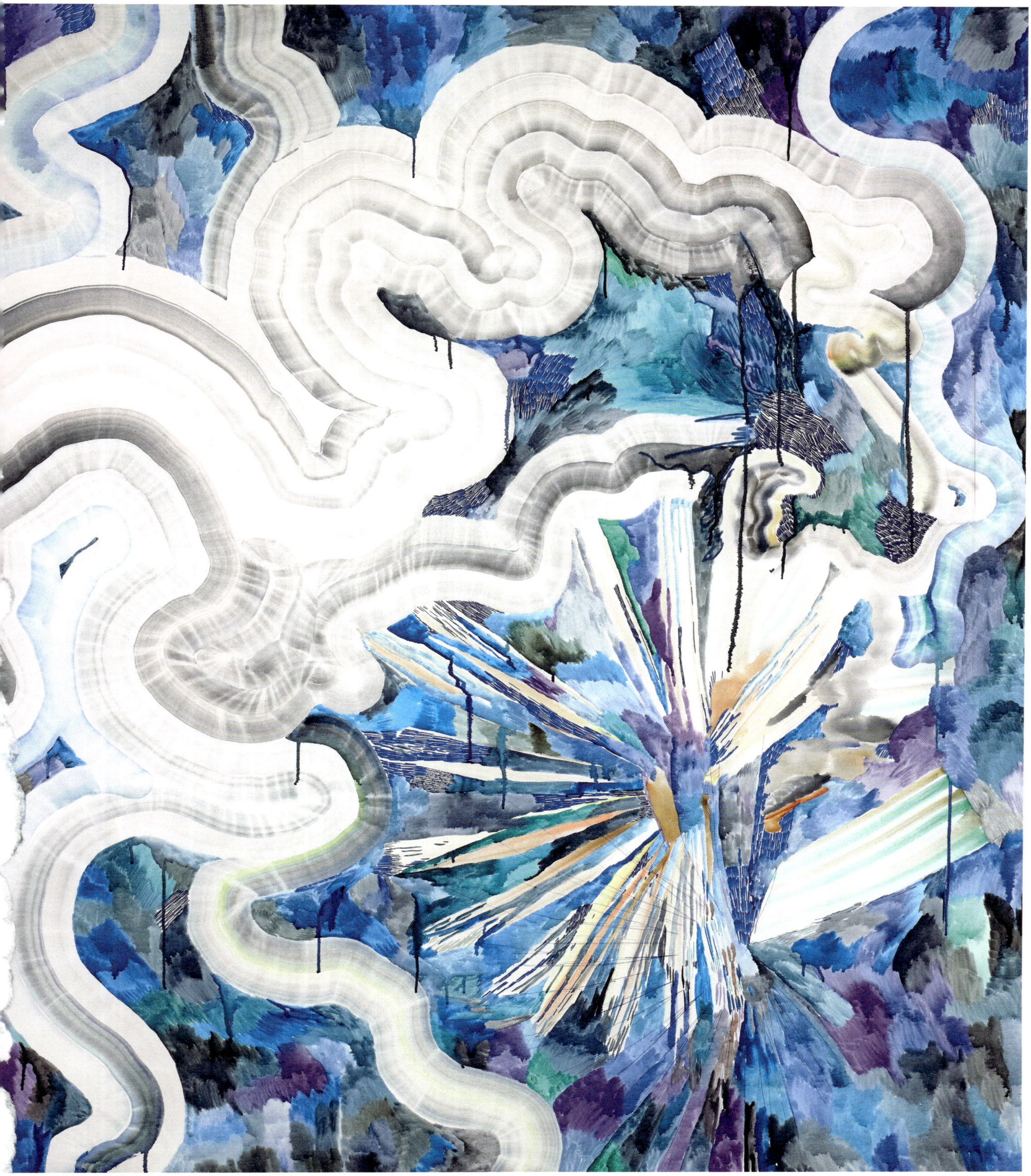

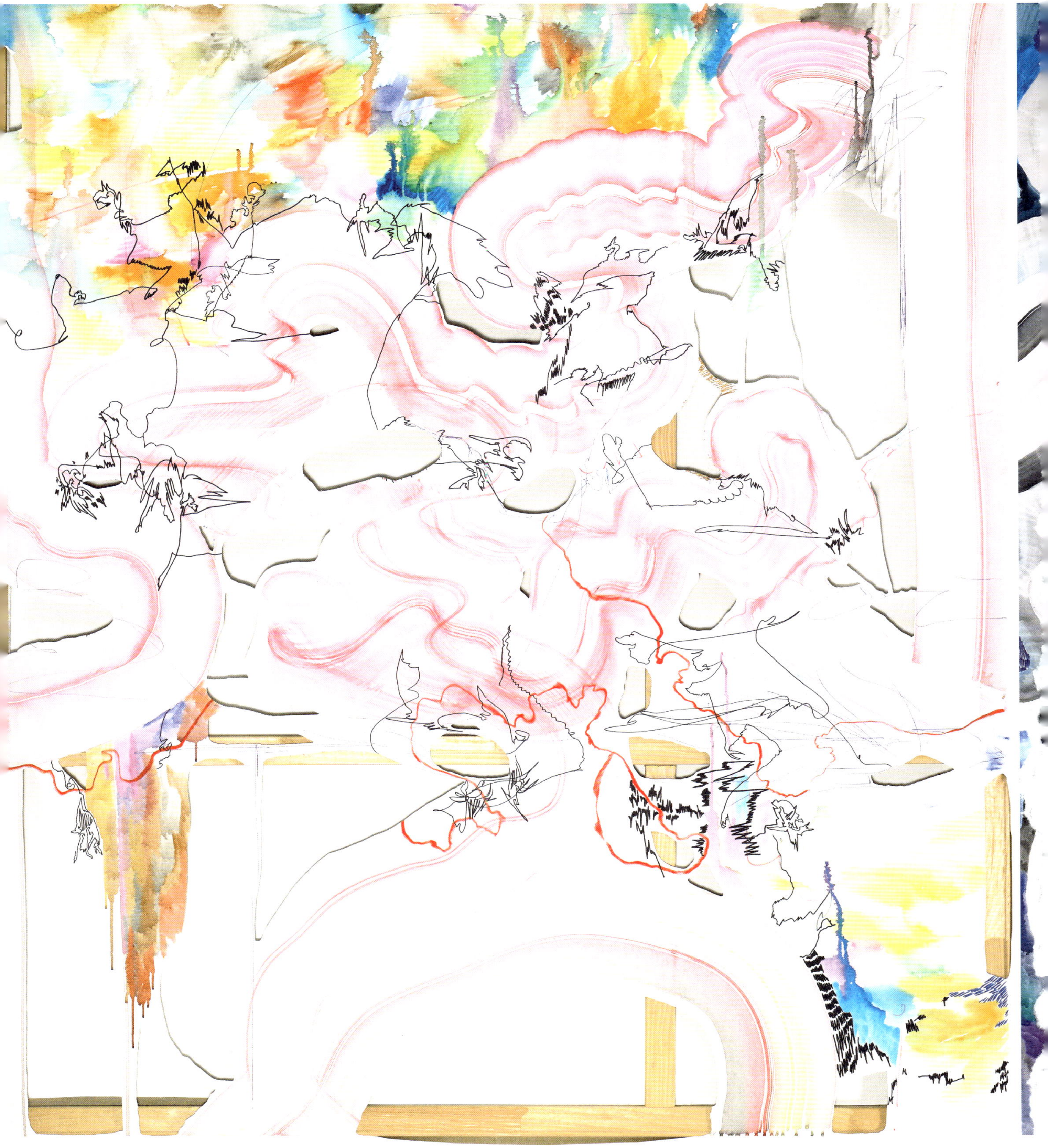

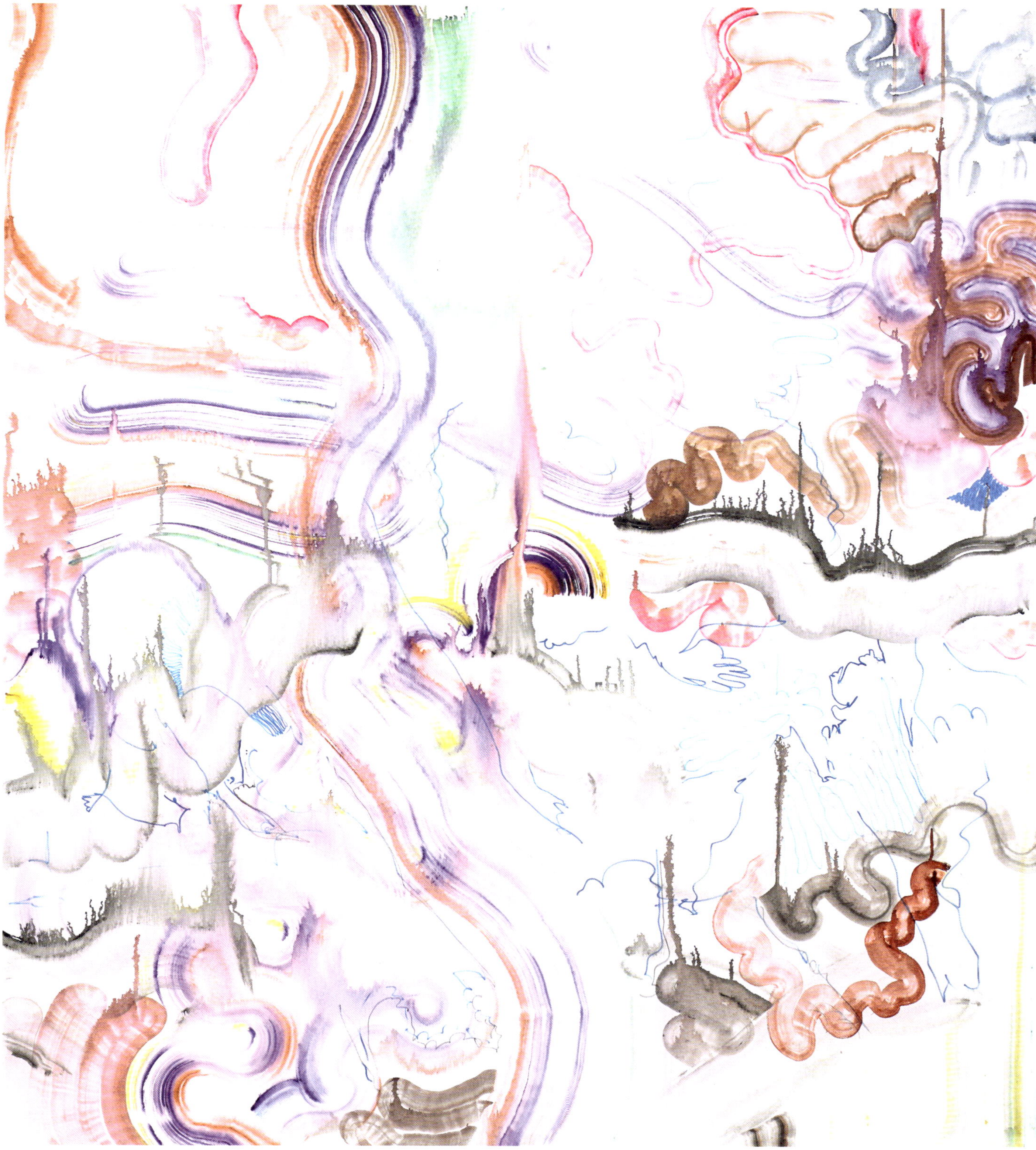

Untitled, watercolour/marker on linen, 170 × 150 cm, 2020

The Self Portraits / Portraits to Questions of Femininity, digital silver gelatin print on baryta paper, original size 10,5 × 15,5 cm, 2001 – ongoing

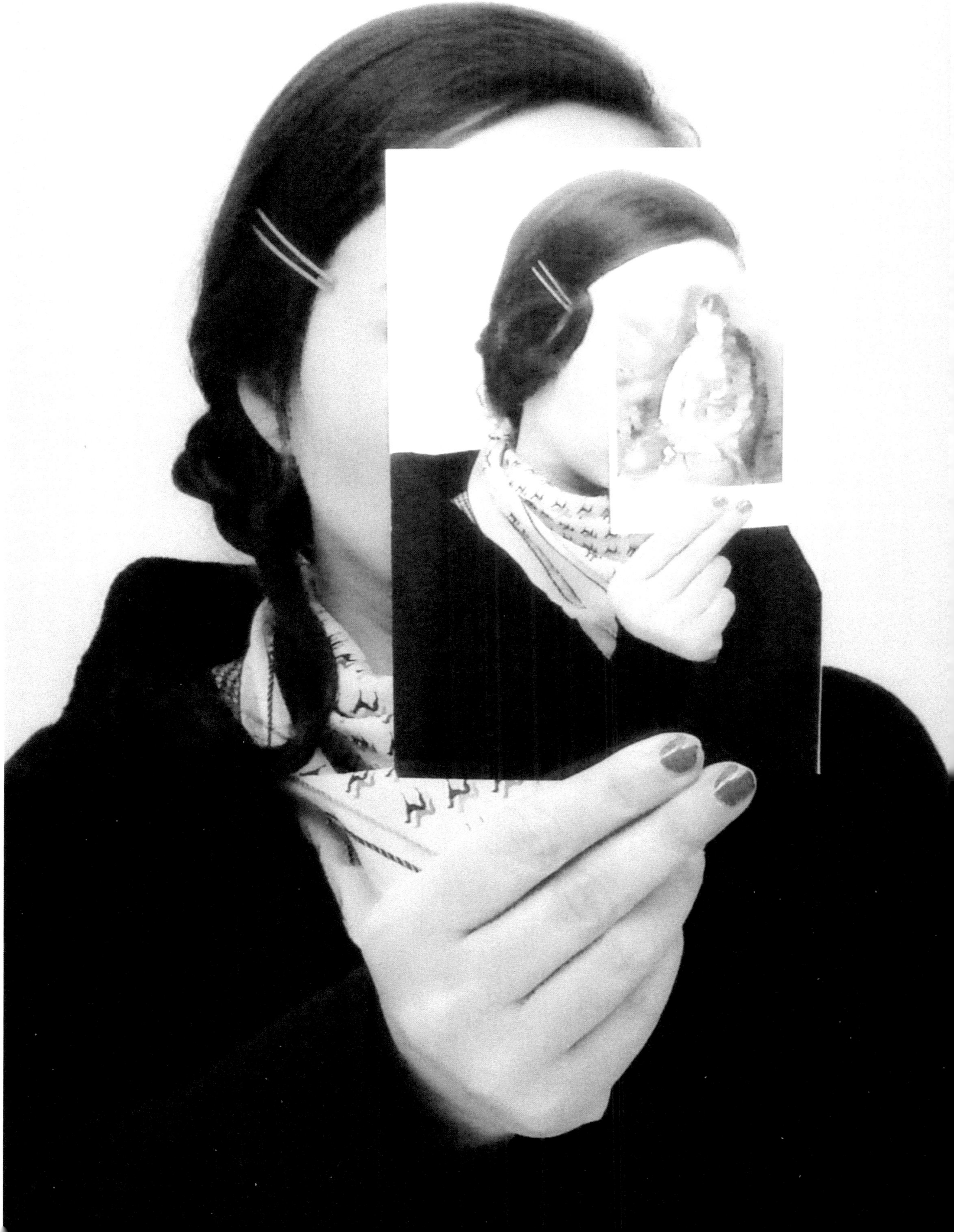

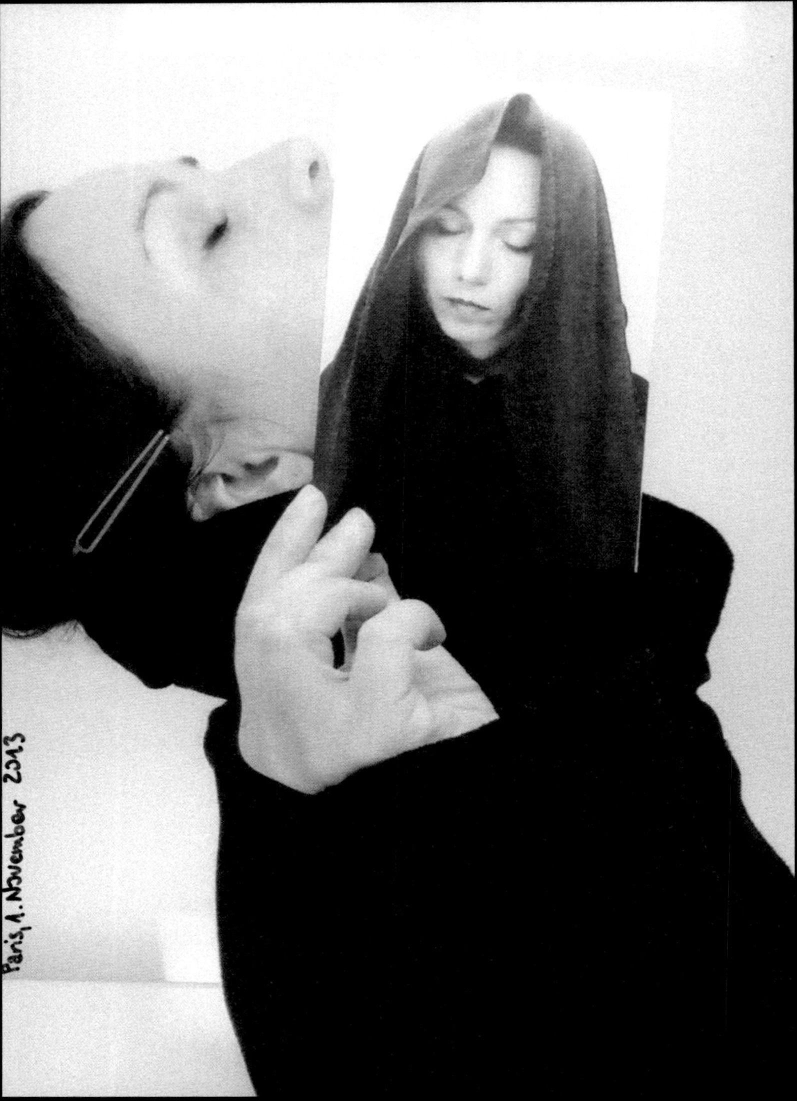

[…] the woman's body is one of the essential elements of the situation she occupies in this world. But her body is not enough to define her; it has a lived reality only as taken on by consciousness through actions and within a society […].[1] —Simone de Beauvoir

By recognizing "our" uncanny strangeness we shall neither suffer from it nor enjoy it from the outside. The foreigner is within me, hence we are all foreigners. If I am a foreigner, there are no foreigners.[2] —Julia Kristeva

Strange indeed is the encounter with the other – whom we perceive by means of sight, hearing, smell, but do not "frame" within our consciousness. The other leaves us separate, incoherent […]. Also strange is the experience of the abyss separating me from the other who shocks me – I do not even perceive him, perhaps he crushes me because I negate him. Confronting the foreigner whom I reject and with whom at the same time I identify, I lose my boundaries, I no longer have a container […]. The uncanny strangeness allows for many variations: they all repeat the difficulty I have in situating myself with respect to the other and keep going over the course of identification-projection that lies at the foundation of my reaching autonomy.[3] —Julia Kristeva

Belle Vie en Navy Blue About Self-Portraits – Looking at the World through the Self

The author of what I describe is not myself, it is the Other. First of all it is you, it is the woman, it is the queen, it is the Child, it is a person who is greater than I and who surpasses you as well, whom you do not know. I am your scribe.[4] —Hélène Cixous

Barbara Rüdiger

[...] when we talk about the body we talk about something entirely opposed to the closed and the finite. With the body, we speak about something open infinite. [...] the body is the open.[5] —Jean-Luc Nancy

The Self Portraits / Portraits to Questions of Femininity is the title of Patricia Reinhart's ongoing series of self-portraits, she has been creating since 2001. This has been a recurring theme for the past two decades: on location in Paris, the artist uses the existing photomatons in the Métro stations to photograph herself. Between stops, such as Porte des Lilas or Pont Neuf, phases of a life are inscribed. They are locations that connect the private with the public space, interweaving them to form an individual world of images. The brief appropriation of a tiny booth – a passport photo machine as *A Room of One's Own*[6] – thus becomes the stage for an intimate moment, featuring a black-and-white photograph as an accomplice to a staged embodiment. But the artist's look inward, in the act of repetition, opens up the expansion of her own identity(ies) – she looks at us by looking at herself, opening the viewer's eyes. Sometimes an amplification takes place because of the duplicated image and gives us a direction of legibility – away from the image of a young woman and onward toward an emphasis on an emancipatory gesture. The distance created by the strictly conceptual approach is transformed into personal closeness by the familiarity of the photographic setting. Format and location are familiar, the process is that of an everyday one: the product, a means to an end or image carrier of private memories, lodged in our imagination somewhere between a passport photo and a display of love. The artist's physical presence becomes a projection surface, her preceding inner monologue serves as a mirror. The self-portraits become a vehicle for female identities. Portrait after portrait and layer after layer, her gestures are condensed in the medium of photography and symbolically inscribe themselves in the visual theme. The narrative strands interlace to form a fabric of social conditions and circumstances. Their balance of power is left to individual observation, for which the visual elements set in relation to each other serve as links to points of reference and departure.

Barbara Rüdiger is a curator for contemporary art. 2003–2008 Studies at the Academy of Fine Arts Vienna. She has worked with institutions such as basis wien, Secession, mumok – Museum moderner Kunst Stiftung Ludwig Wien as well as the Institute of Science and Technology Austria.

1 Simone de Beauvoir, *The Second Sex* (1949), New York 2009, p. 71.
2 Julia Kristeva, *Strangers to Ourselves* (1988), New York 1991, p. 192.
3 Ibid., p. 187.
4 Hélène Cixous, *The Book of Promethea* (1983), London 1991, p. 208.
5 Jean-Luc Nancy, "On the Soul", in: id., Corpus (2000), New York 2008, p. 122.
6 Virginia Woolf, *A Room of One's Own*, London 1929.

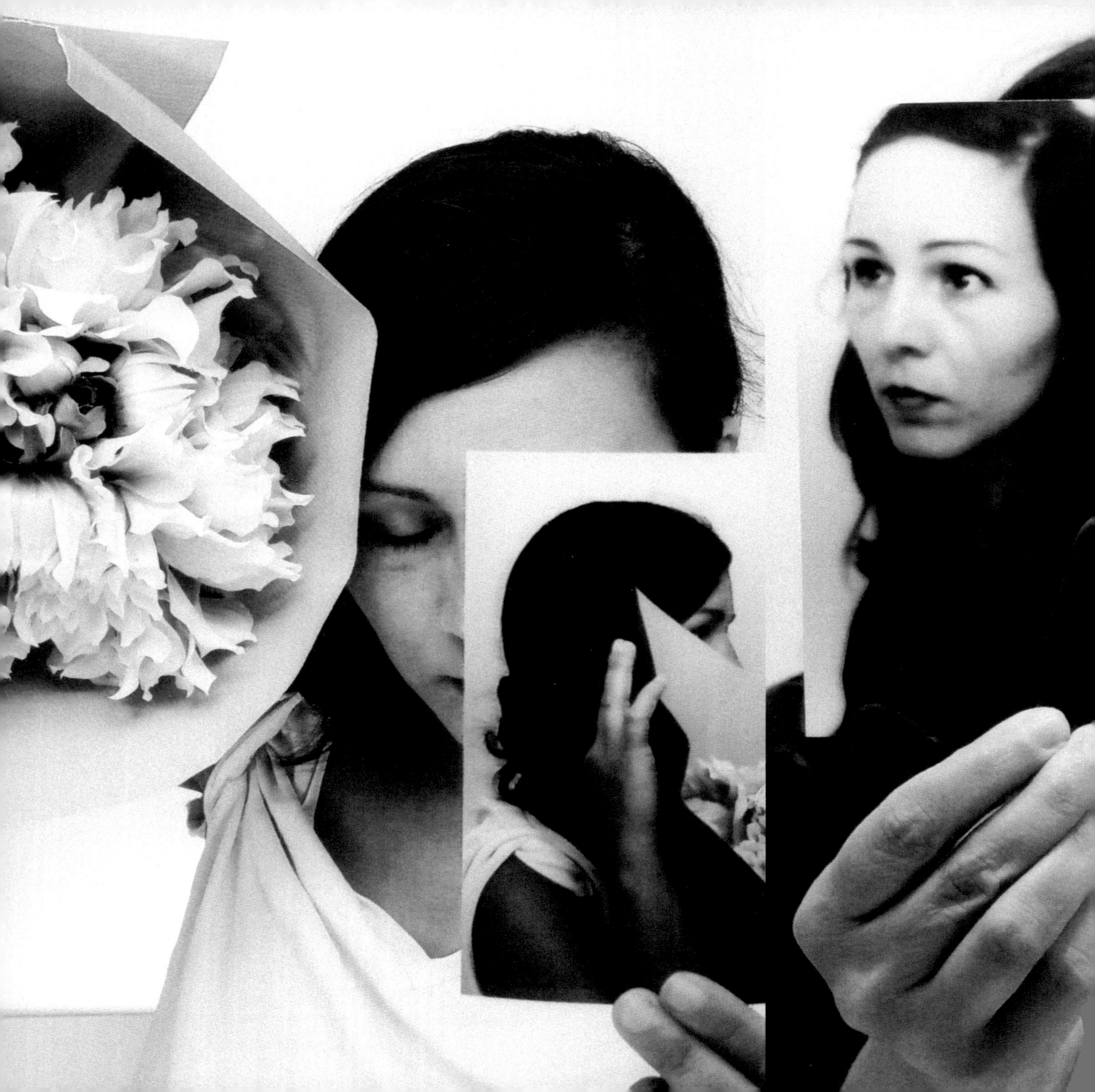

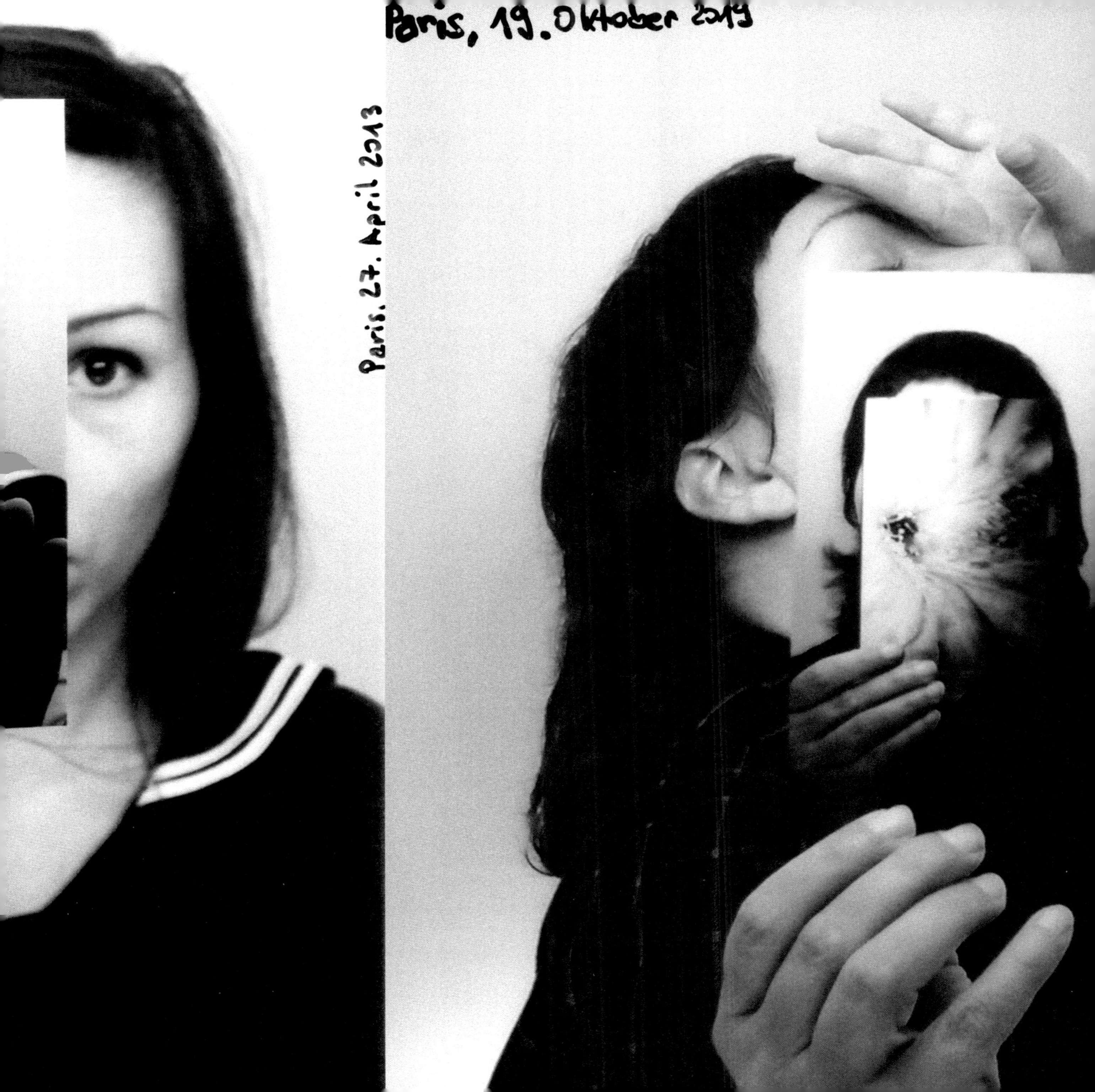
Paris, 19. Oktober 2019
Paris, 27. April 2013

Belle Vie en Navy Blue Über Selbstbildnisse – ein Blick auf die Welt durch das Ich

Die Autorin, die ich beschreibe, bin nicht ich, es ist DIE ANDERE. Du bist es, zuerst, die Frau ist es, die Königin, DAS Kind, eine Person, die viel größer ist als ich und die auch über dich hinausgeht, und die du nicht kennst. Ich bin deine Schreiberin.[1] — Hélène Cixous

Barbara Rüdiger

[...] wenn wir vom Körper sprechen, sprechen wir von dem, was genau das Gegenteil des Geschlossenen und Abgeschlossenen ist. [...] Der Körper ist das Offene.[2] — Jean-Luc Nancy

The Self Portraits / Portraits to Questions of Femininity ist der Titel der seit 2001 entstehenden fortlaufenden Serie an Selbstporträts von Patricia Reinhart. Seit mittlerweile zwei Dekaden basiert diese Werkreihe auf einem sich wiederholenden Prinzip: Vor Ort in Paris nutzt die Künstlerin die Photomatons in den Stationen der Métro, um sich darin ablichten zu lassen. Zwischen den Haltestellen – von Porte des Lilas bis Pont Neuf – schreiben sich Stationen eines Lebens ein. Sie sind Standorte, die das Private mit dem öffentlichen Raum verbinden und sich zu einer individuellen Bilderwelt verweben. Die nur kurze Aneignung der winzigen Kabine eines Passbildautomaten als *A Room of One's Own*[3] wird zur Bühne eines intimen Moments, die Schwarz-Weiß-Fotografie zur Komplizin einer inszenierten Verkörperung. Doch der vermeintliche Blick der Künstlerin auf sich selbst eröffnet im Akt der Wiederholung eine Ausdehnung der eigenen Identität(en) – sie blickt uns an, indem sie sich selbst erblickt, und öffnet den Betrachter:innen die Augen. Manchmal findet durch die Verdoppelung einer Abbildung eine Verstärkung statt und gibt uns eine Richtung für die Lesbarkeit vor – weg vom Abbild einer jungen Frau, hin zur Betonung einer Geste des Emanzipatorischen.

Die durch die streng konzeptuelle Vorgangsweise entstehende Distanz wandelt sich angesichts der Vertrautheit des fotografischen Settings in persönliche Nähe. Format und Ort sind uns bekannt, der Vorgang ist ein alltäglicher: das Produkt als ein Mittel zum Zweck oder als Träger privater Bilderinnerungen, zwischen Passfoto und Liebesbezeigung. Die physische Präsenz der Künstlerin wird zu einer Projektionsfläche, ihr vorausgegangener innerer Monolog dient uns als Spiegel. Die Selbstbildnisse werden zum Träger für weibliche Identitäten. Porträt um Porträt und Lage um Lage verdichten sich Reinharts Gesten im Medium der Fotografie und schreiben sich symbolisch ins Bildmotiv mit ein. Die Erzählstränge verketten sich zu einem Gewebe aus sozialen Zuständen und Umständen. Ihr Kräfteverhältnis obliegt der individuellen Betrachtung, als Querverweise zu Anhalts- und Ausgangspunkten dienen dabei die zueinander in Bezug gesetzten Gestaltungselemente.

Barbara Rüdiger ist Kuratorin für zeitgenössische Kunst. 2003–2008 Studium an der Akademie der bildenden Künste Wien. Sie arbeitete unter anderem mit Institutionen wie der basis wien, der Secession und dem mumok – Museum moderner Kunst Stiftung Ludwig Wien sowie dem Institute of Science and Technology Austria.

1 Hélène Cixous, *Das Buch von Promethea* (1983), Wien 1990, S. 238.
2 Jean-Luc Nancy, „Über die Seele", in: ders., *Corpus* (2000), Zürich 2014, S. 121.
3 Virginia Woolf, *Ein Zimmer für sich allein* (1929), Berlin 1978.
4 Simone de Beauvoir, *Das andere Geschlecht. Sitte und Sexus der Frau* (1949), Hamburg 1951, S. 62.
5 Julia Kristeva, *Fremde sind wir uns selbst* (1988), Frankfurt am Main 1990, S. 209.
6 Ebd., S. 209.

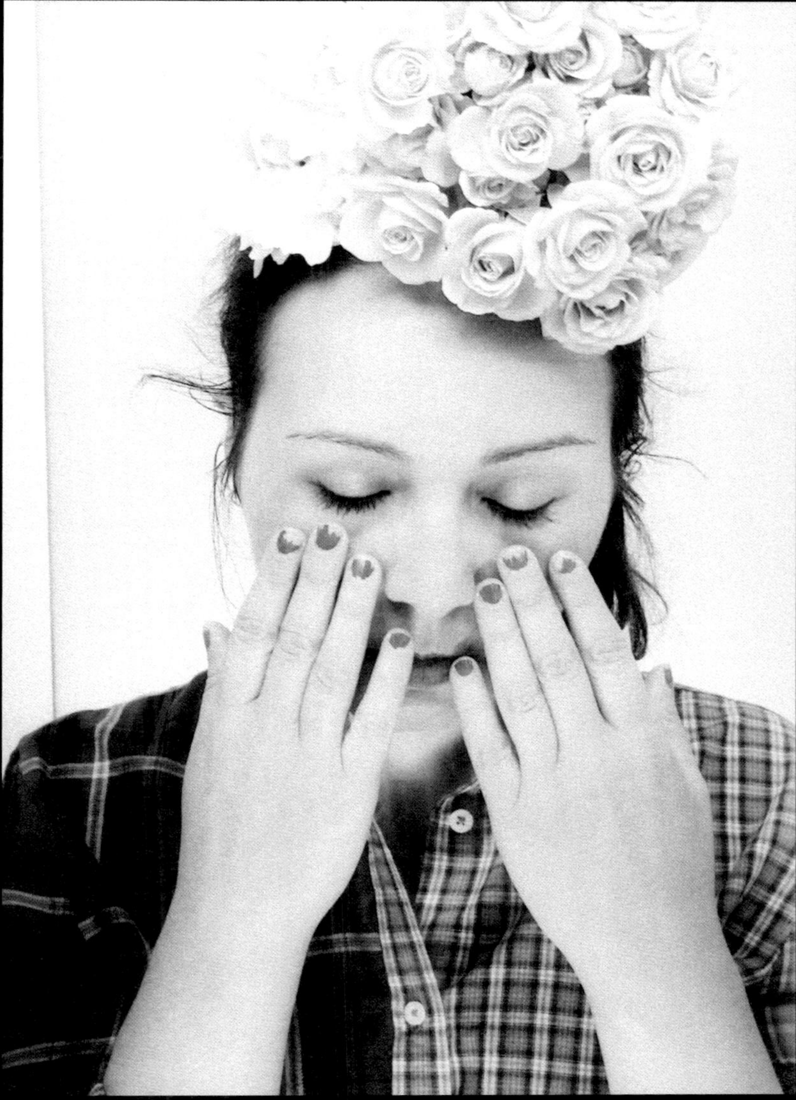

[...] der Körper der Frau ist eines der wesentlichen Elemente für die Situation, die sie in der Welt einnimmt. Aber andererseits genügt er auch nicht, um sie zu definieren; er hat nur gelebte Realität, sofern er vom Bewußtsein durch Handlungen und innerhalb einer Gesellschaft bejaht wird [...].[4] — Simone de Beauvoir

Wenn wir „unsere" Fremdheit erkennen, werden wir draußen weder unter ihr leiden noch sie genießen. Das Fremde ist in mir, also sind wir alle Fremde. Wenn ich Fremder bin, gibt es keine Fremden.[5] — Julia Kristeva

Sie ist in der Tat seltsam, die Begegnung mit dem anderen – den wir durch den Blick, das Gehör, den Geruchssinn wahrnehmen, aber nicht bewusst „erfassen". Der andere läßt uns getrennt, zusammenhanglos zurück [...]. Seltsam auch diese Erfahrung des Abgrunds zwischen mir und dem anderen, der mich schockiert – ich nehme ihn nicht einmal wahr, vielleicht vernichtet er mich, weil ich ihn leugne. Angesichts des Fremden, den ich ablehne und mit dem ich mich identifiziere, beides zugleich, lösen sich meine festgefügten Grenzen auf, meine Konturen zerfließen [...]. Die Varianten des Unheimlichen, der beunruhigenden Fremdheit sind vielfältig: alle wiederholen meine Schwierigkeit, mich im Verhältnis zum anderen zu situieren, und eröffnen noch einmal den Weg der Identifikation-Projektion, der am Grund meines Aufstiegs zur Autonomie liegt.[6] — Julia Kristeva

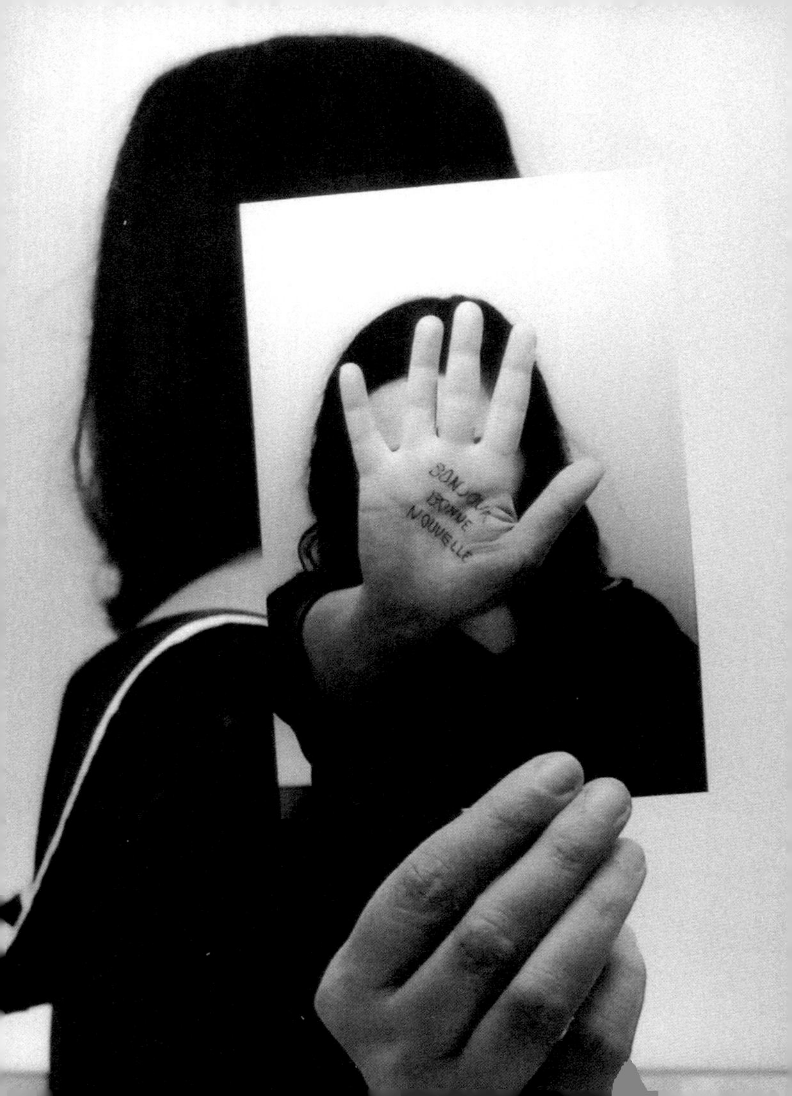
BONNE
NOUVELLE

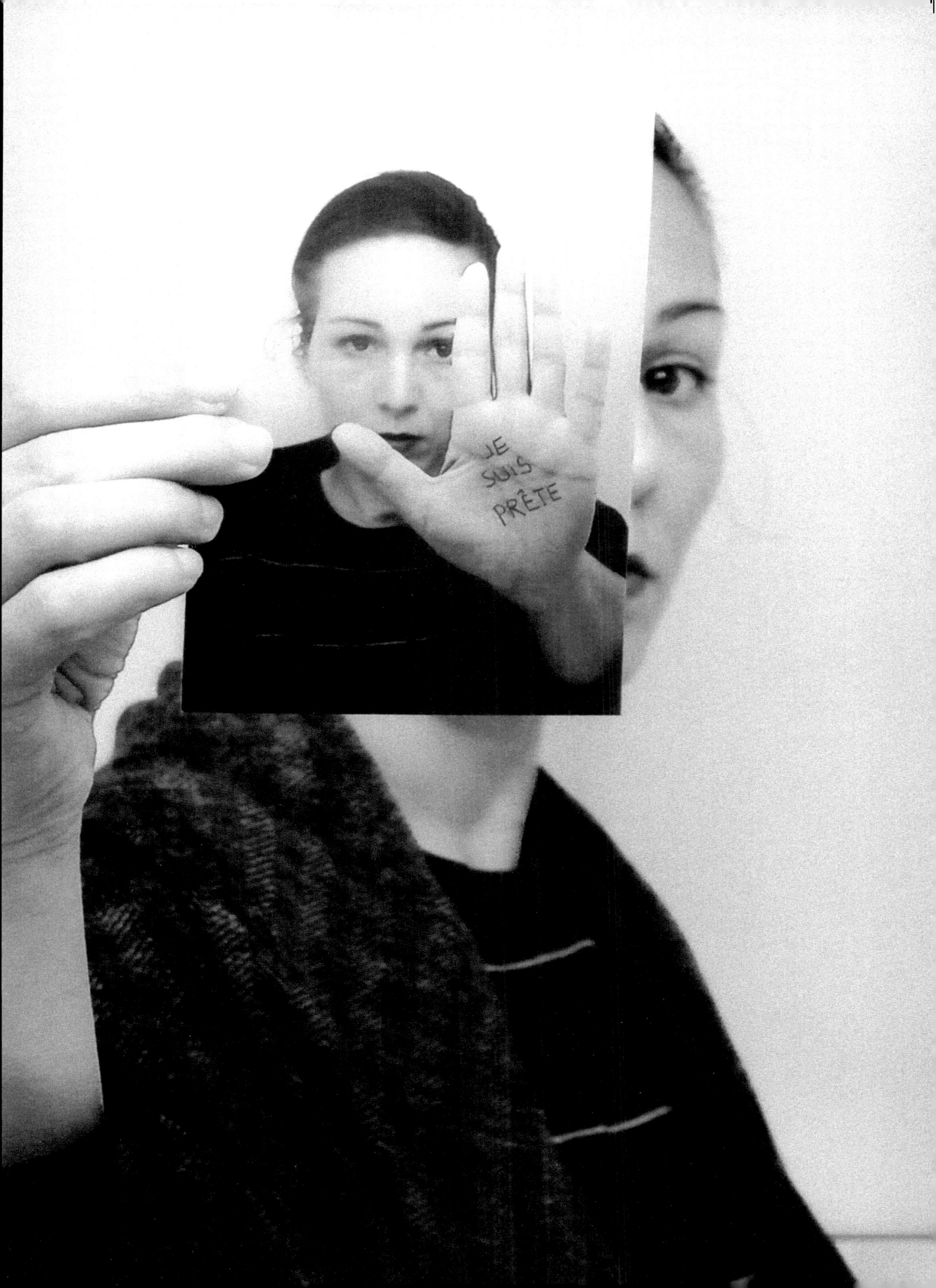
JE
SUIS
PRÊTE

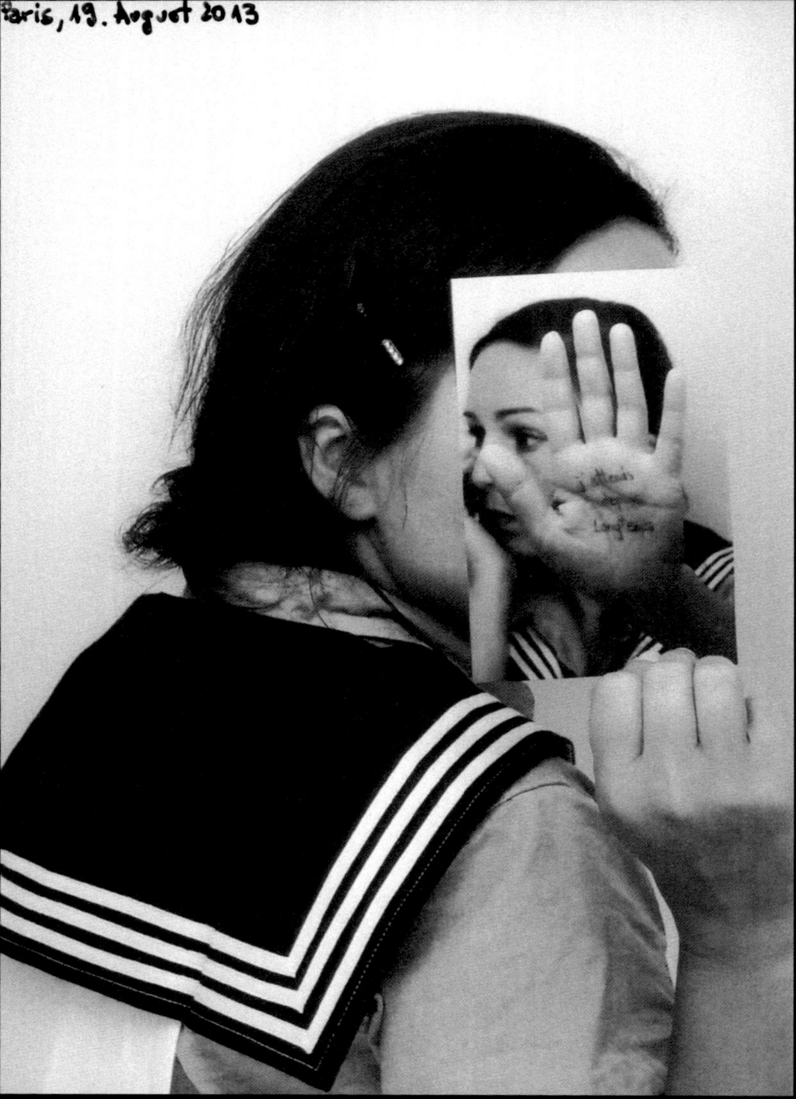

[...] le corps de la femme est un des éléments essentiels de la situation qu'elle occupe dans le monde. Mais ce n'est pas non plus lui qui suffit à la définir ; il n'a de réalité vécue qu'en tant qu'assumé par la conscience à travers des actions et au sein d'une société [...].[1] — Simone de Beauvoir

À reconnaître « notre » inquiétante étrangeté, nous n'en souffrirons ni n'en jouirons de dehors. L'étrange est en moi, donc nous sommes tous des étrangers. Si je suis étranger, il n'y a pas d'étrangers.[2] — Julia Kristeva

Étrange, en effet, la rencontre avec l'autre – que nous percevons par la vue, l'ouïe, l'odorat, mais n'« encadrons » pas par la conscience. L'autre nous laisse séparés, incohérents [...]. Étrange aussi, cette expérience de l'abîme entre moi et l'autre qui me choque – je ne le perçois même pas, il m'annihile peut-être parce que je le nie. Face à l'étranger que je refuse et auquel je m'identifie à la fois, je perds mes limites, je n'ai plus de contenants [...]. Multiples sont les variantes de l'inquiétante étrangeté : toutes réitèrent ma difficulté à me placer par rapport à l'autre et refont le trajet de l'identification-projection qui gît au fondement de mon accession à l'autonomie.[3] — Julia Kristeva

Belle Vie en Navy Blue Des autoportraits – regarder le monde à travers le Soi

L'auteur de ce que je décris, ce n'est pas moi, c'est l'Autre. C'est toi d'abord, c'est la femme, c'est la reine, c'est l'Enfant, c'est une personne plus grande que moi et qui te dépasse aussi, et que tu ne connais pas. Je suis ta scribe.[4] —Hélène Cixous

Barbara Rüdiger

[…] si nous parlons du corps, nous parlons de ce qui est tout le contraire du clos et du fini. Avec le corps, nous parlons de ce qui est ouvert et infini. […] le corps, c'est l'ouvert.[5] —Jean-Luc Nancy

The Self Portraits / Portraits to Questions of Femininity, tel est le titre de la série continue d'autoportraits que Patricia Reinhart réalise depuis 2001. Elle repose depuis deux décennies sur la répétition d'un même principe : l'artiste utilise les photomatons des stations de métro parisiennes pour se photographier. Entre Porte des Lilas et Pont Neuf s'inscrivent ainsi les stations d'une vie. Ce sont des lieux qui nouent la sphère privée et l'espace public, les tissant en un monde personnel d'images. L'appropriation si brève de la minuscule cabine d'un photomaton comme *A Room of One's Own*[6] devient ainsi la scène d'un moment intime, et la photographie en noir et blanc se fait complice d'une incarnation mise en scène. Pourtant, la répétition du prétendu regard sur soi de l'artiste engendre l'expansion de sa propre identité, de ses identités : elle nous regarde en se regardant, ouvrant les yeux du spectateur. Parfois, la duplication d'une image renforce le propos et nous indique un sens de lecture – on s'éloigne de l'image d'une jeune femme pour se rapprocher d'un geste d'émancipation.

La distance créée par une démarche strictement conceptuelle se mue en proximité intime grâce à la familiarité du cadre photographique. Le format et le lieu nous sont connus, le procédé s'inscrit dans notre vie quotidienne. Le produit est à la foi un moyen de parvenir à une fin et une image vectrice de souvenirs personnels, entre photo d'identité et déclaration d'amour. La présence physique de l'artiste devient une surface de projection. Son monologue intérieur, précédant la prise, nous sert de miroir. Les autoportraits se font le support d'identités féminines. Portrait après portrait, situation après situation, ses gestes se condensent dans le médium de la photographie et s'inscrivent symboliquement dans le scénario visuel. Les fils narratifs s'enchaînent en tressant un tissu de conditions sociales et de circonstances. La compréhension des rapports de force est laissée à l'individu qui observe et les éléments visuels définis en relation les uns aux autres sont à la fois des points de repère et des points de départ.

Barbara Rüdiger est commissaire d'exposition d'art contemporain. 2003–2008 : études à l'Académie des Beaux-Arts de Vienne. Elle a travaillé avec des institutions telles que basis wien, la Sécession, le mumok – Museum moderner Kunst Stiftung Ludwig Wien ainsi que l'Institute of Science and Technology Austria.

1 Simone de Beauvoir, *Le deuxième sexe* (1949), Paris 1976, p. 78–79.
2 Julia Kristeva, *Étrangers à nous-mêmes*, Paris 1988, p. 284.
3 Ibid., p. 276.
4 Hélène Cixous, *Le livre de Promethea*, Paris 1983, p. 267.
5 Jean-Luc Nancy, » De l'âme «, dans : id., *Corpus* (2000), Paris 2006, p. 107.
6 Virginia Woolf, *Une chambre à soi* (1929), Paris 1951.

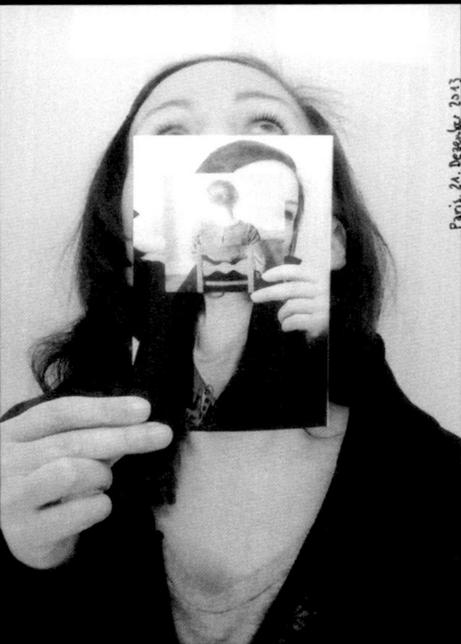
Paris, 21. Dezember 2013
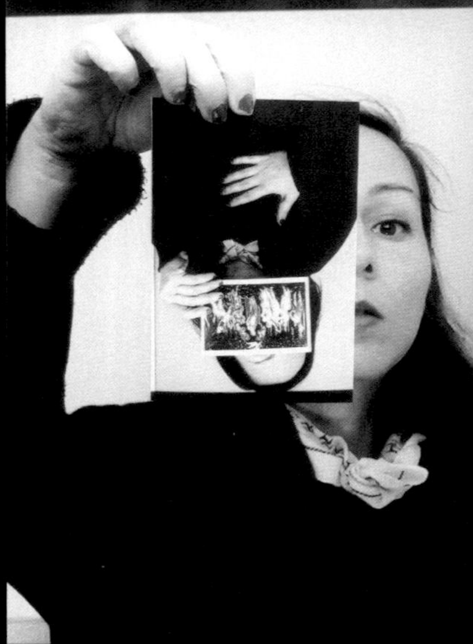
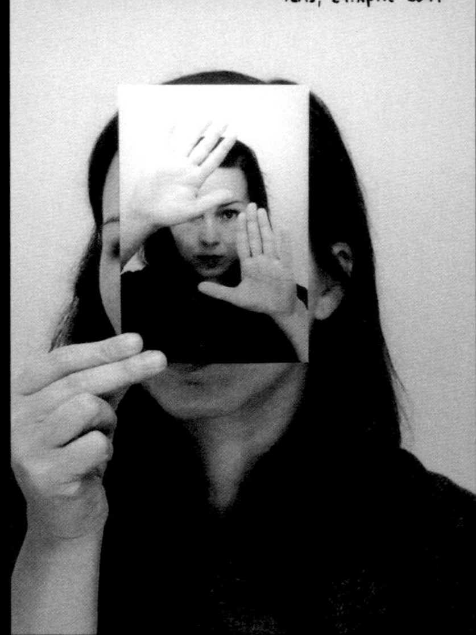
Paris, 24. April 2014
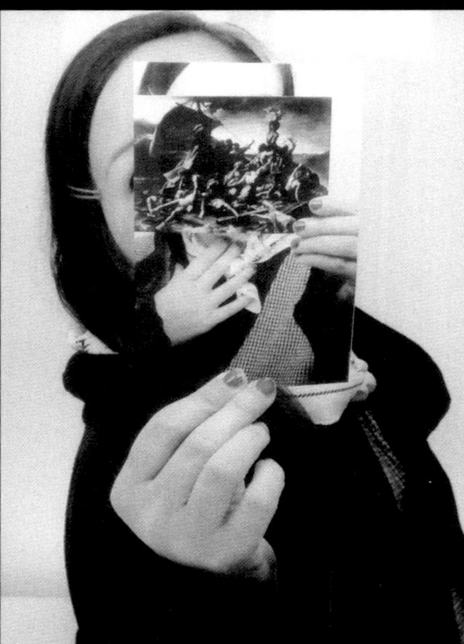
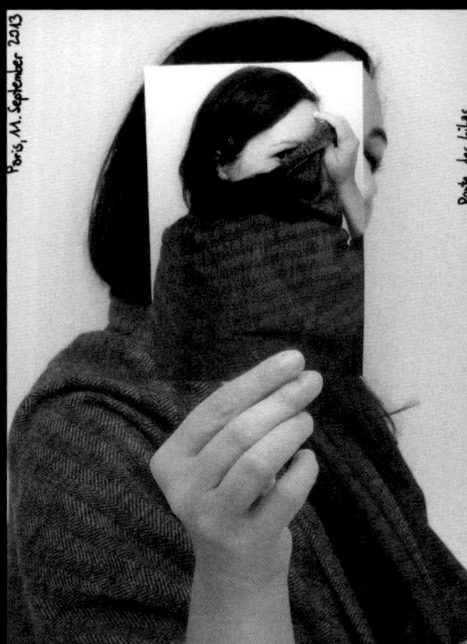
Porte des Lilas
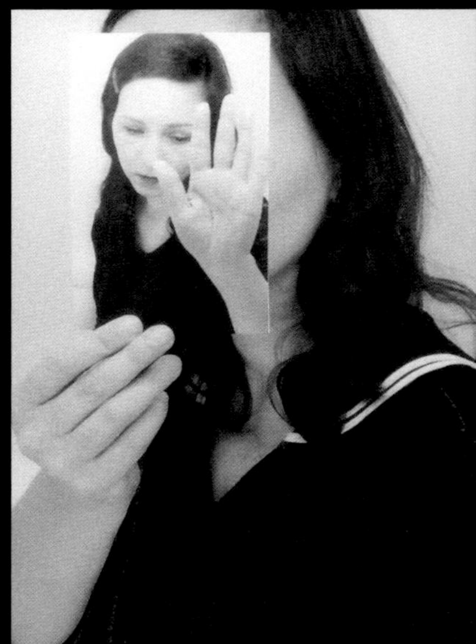
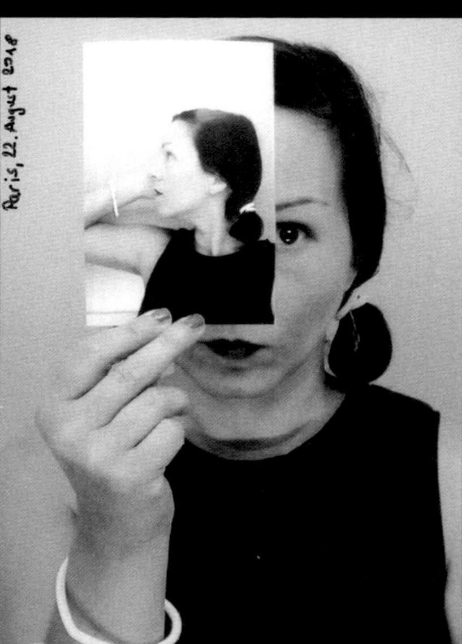
Paris, 22. August 2018
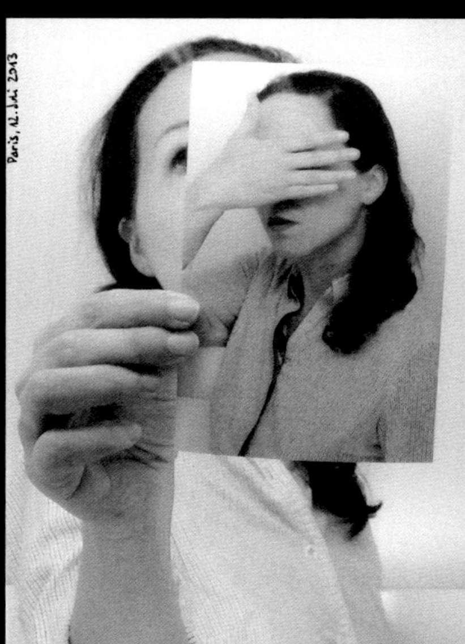
Paris, 12. Juli 2013
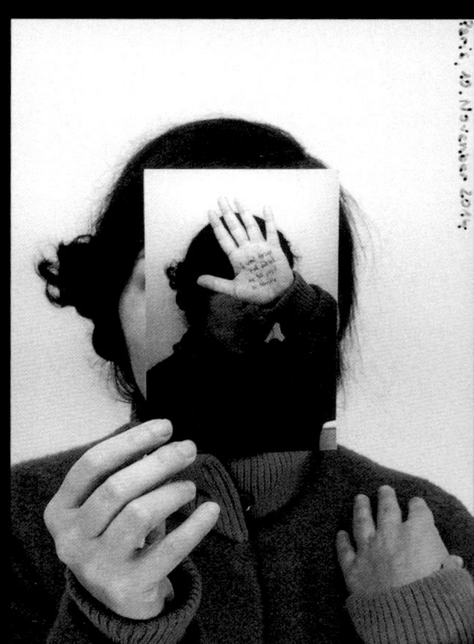

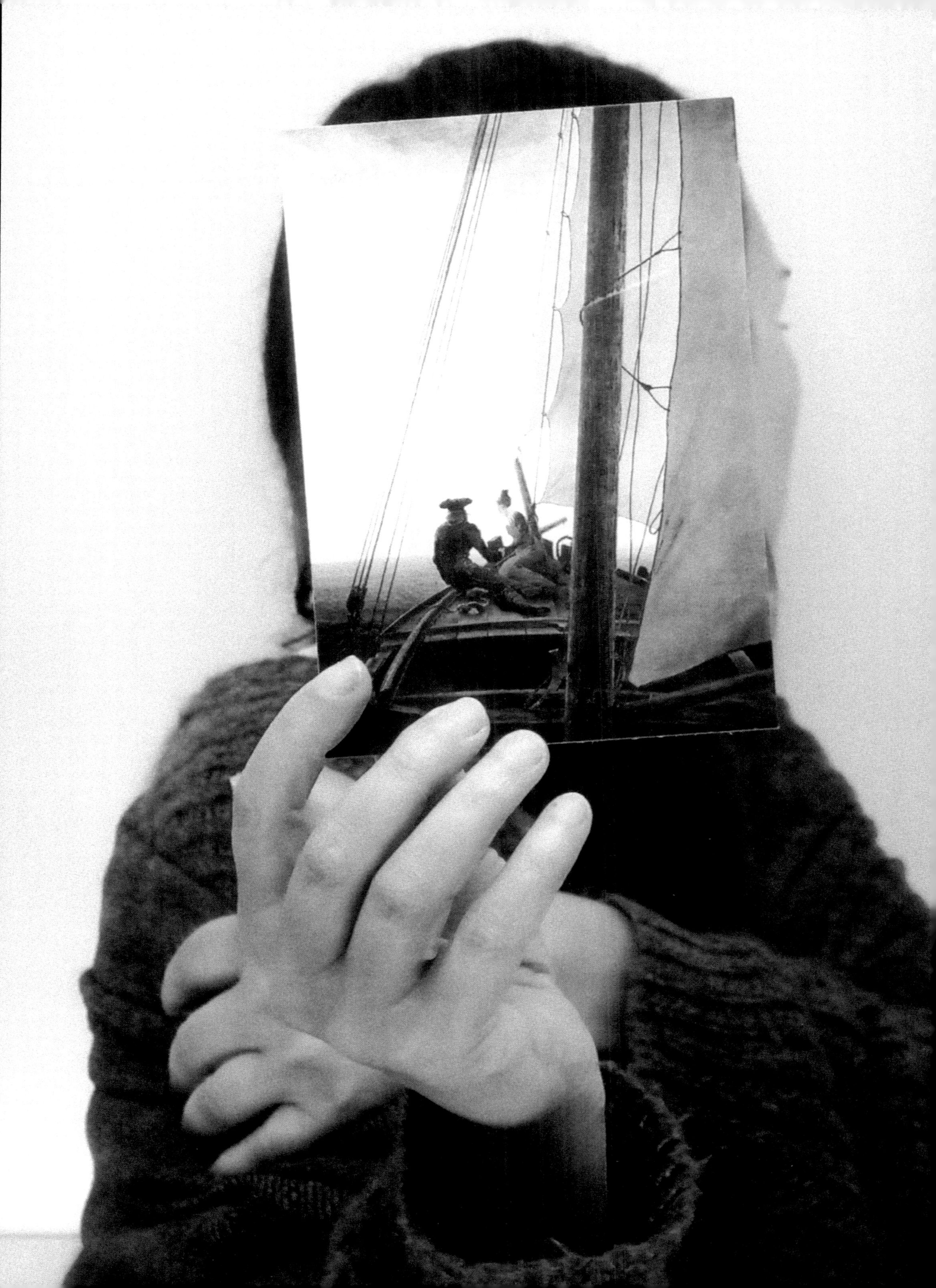

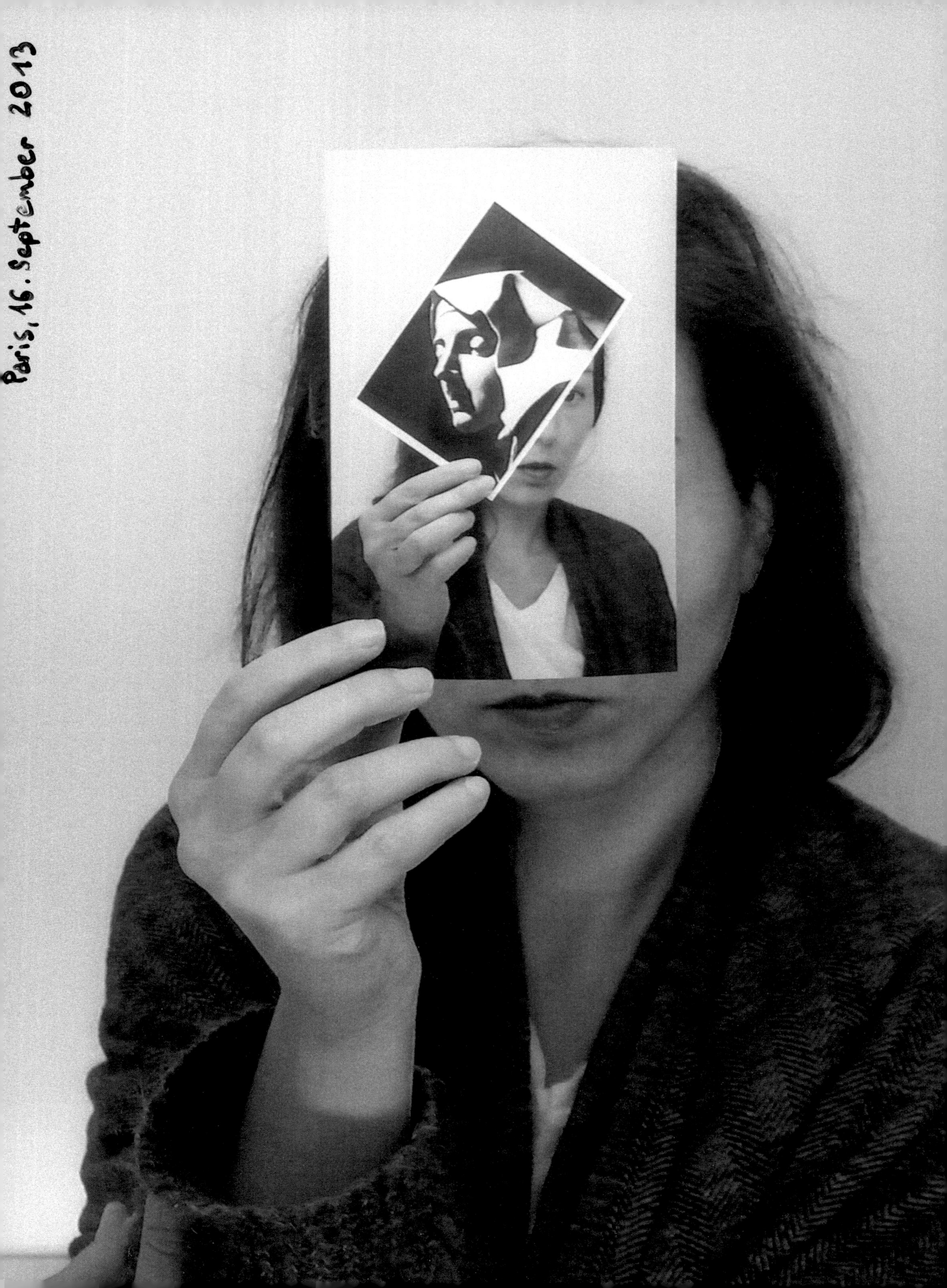
Paris, 16. September 2013

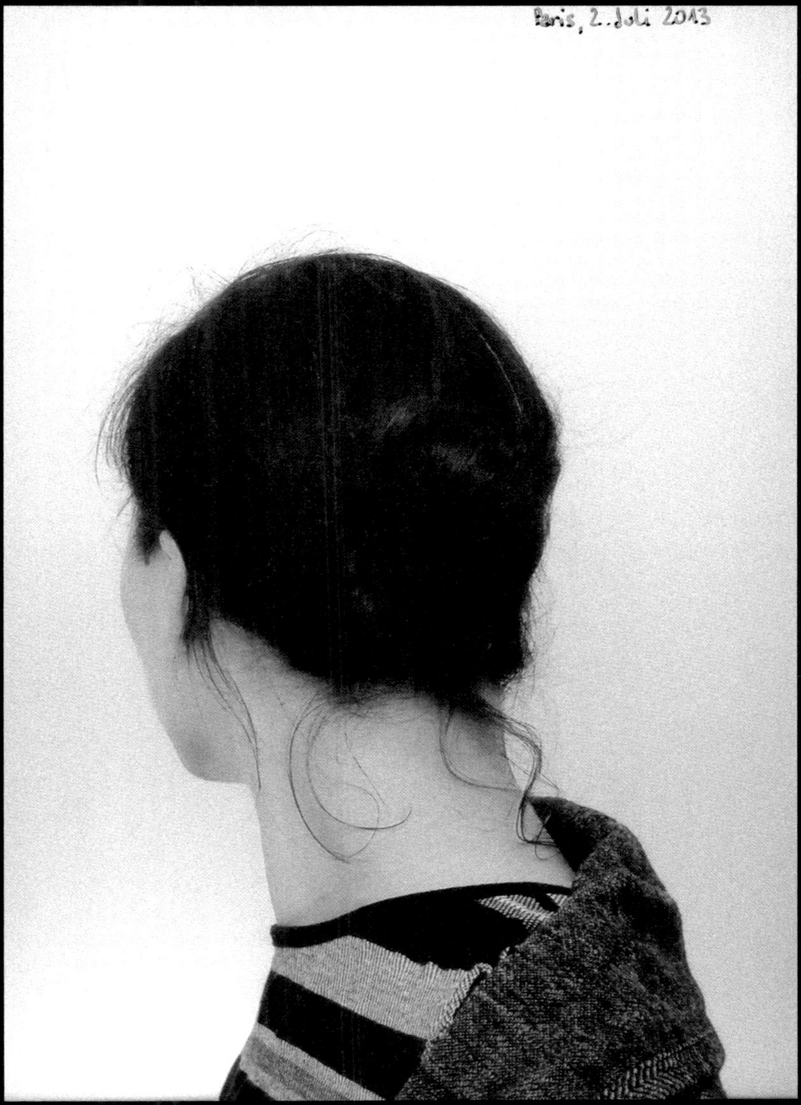

As a woman, after the storm, I lay down my arms.
I don't want to fight anymore or to act like a man.
I would love to go to the garden, as a woman.

Als eine Frau, nach dem Sturm, lege ich meine Waffen nieder.
Ich will nicht mehr kämpfen oder mich wie ein Mann verhalten.
Ich möchte gerne in den Garten gehen, als eine Frau.

En tant que femme, après la tempête, je dépose mes armes.
Je ne veux plus me battre ni agir comme un homme.
J'aimerais aller au jardin, comme une femme.

—Patricia Reinhart

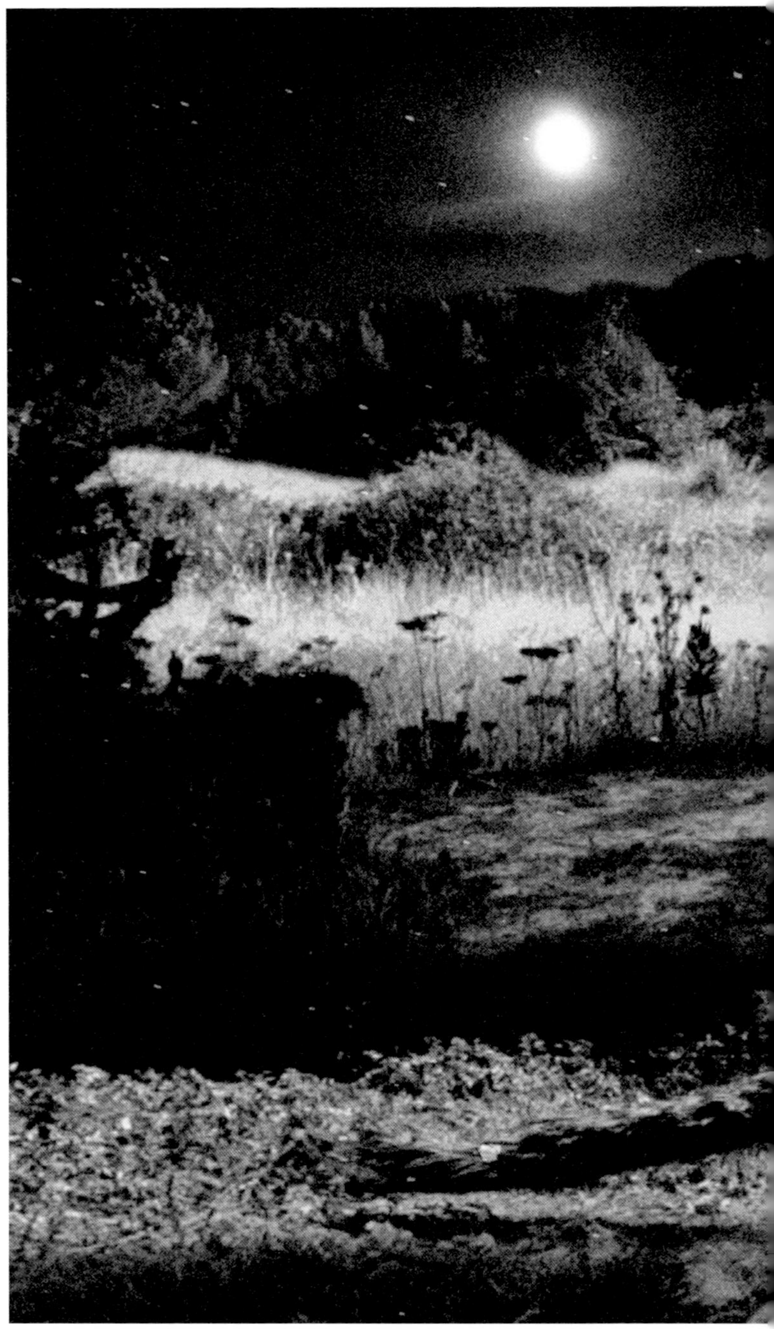

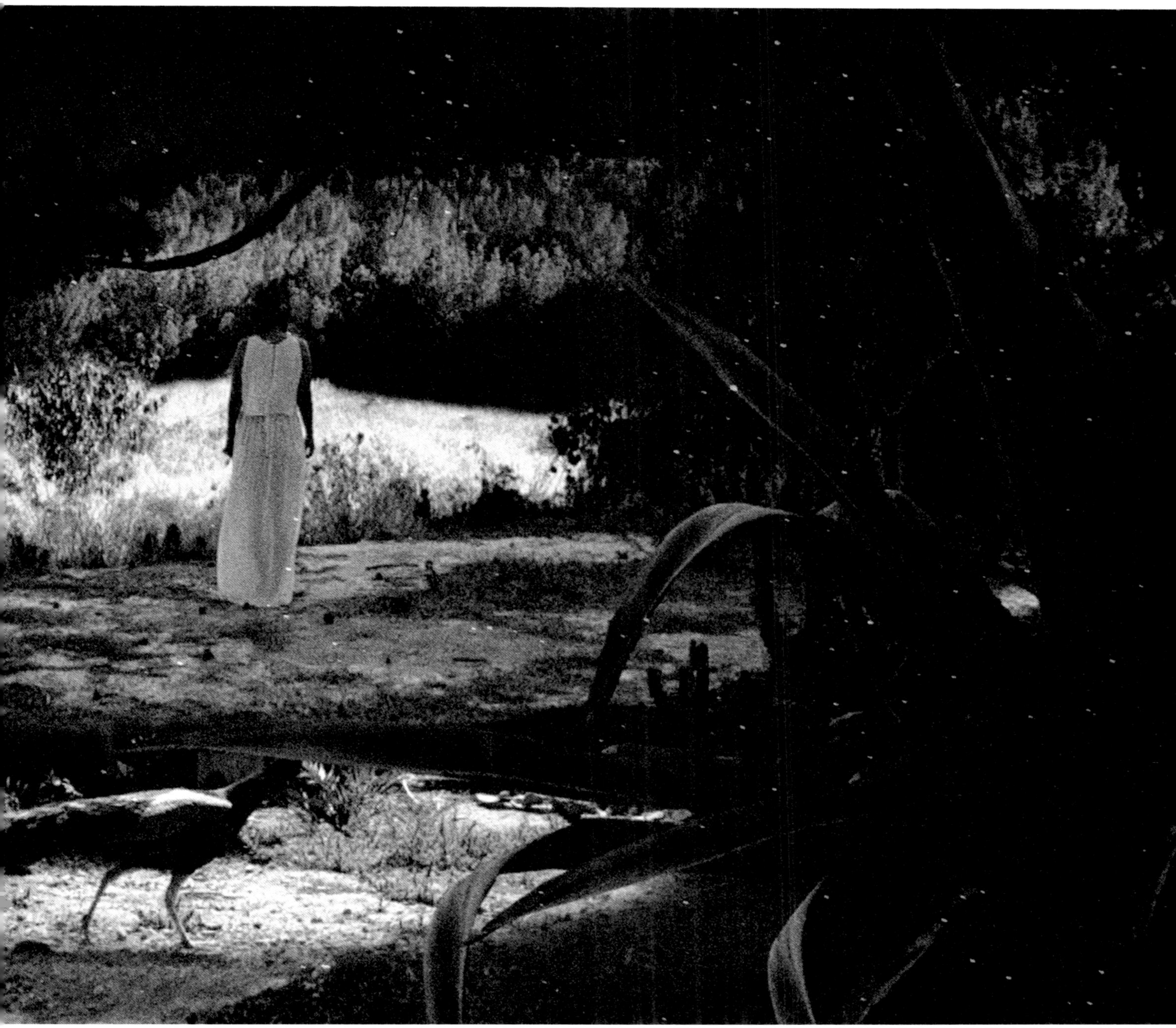

Anoir and the Woman in the Garden, Ciné Collage, 2015–2017

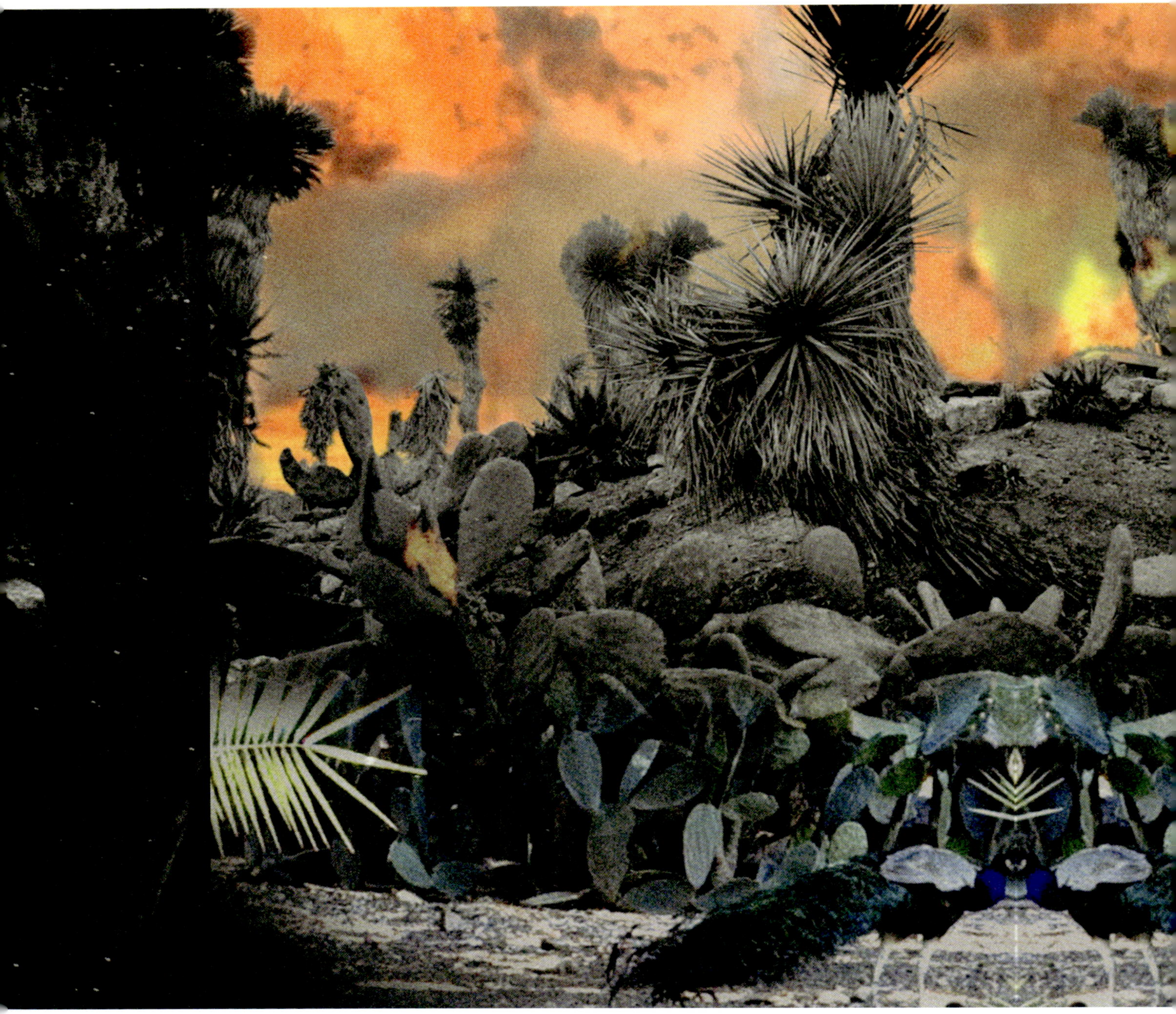

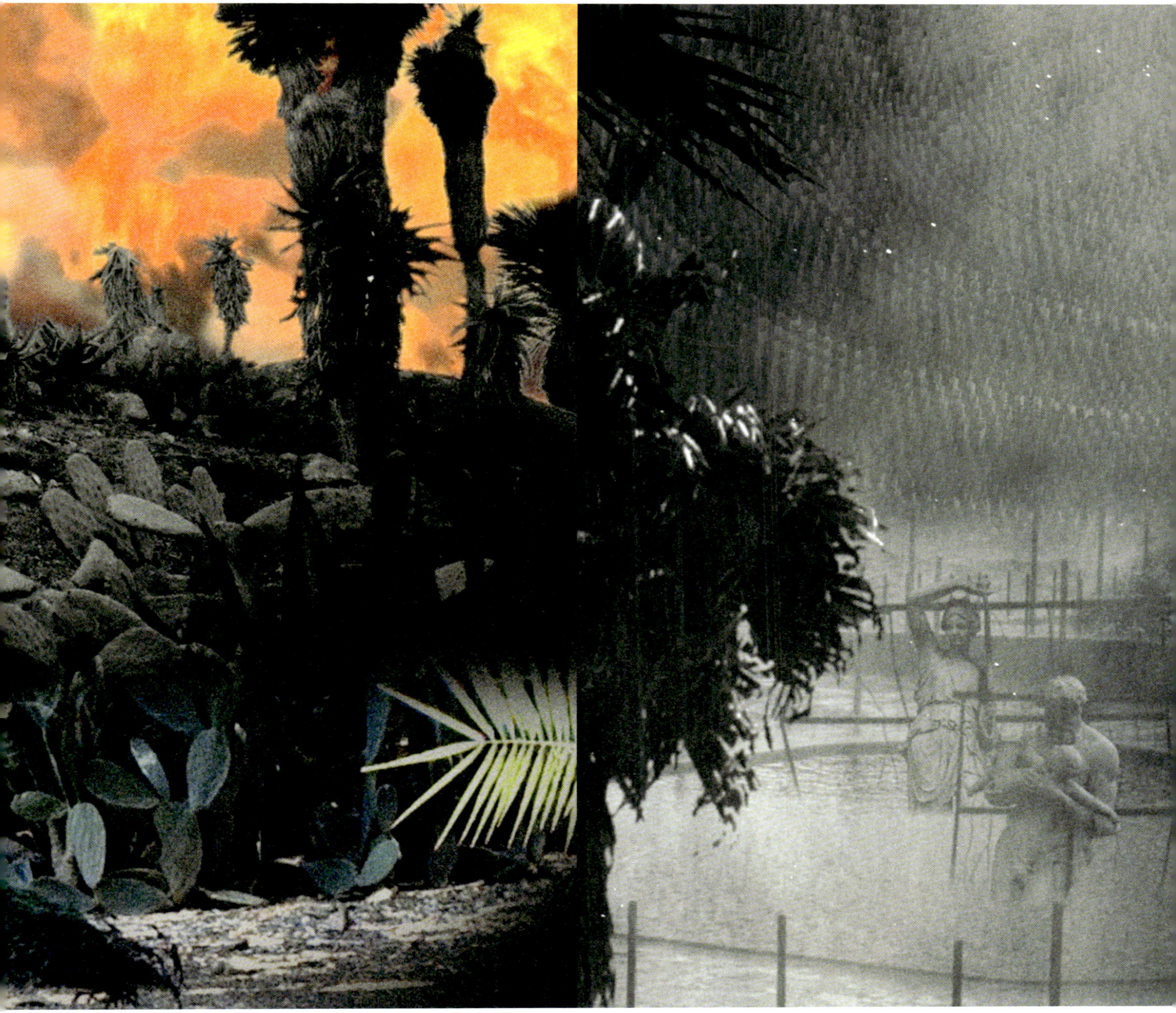

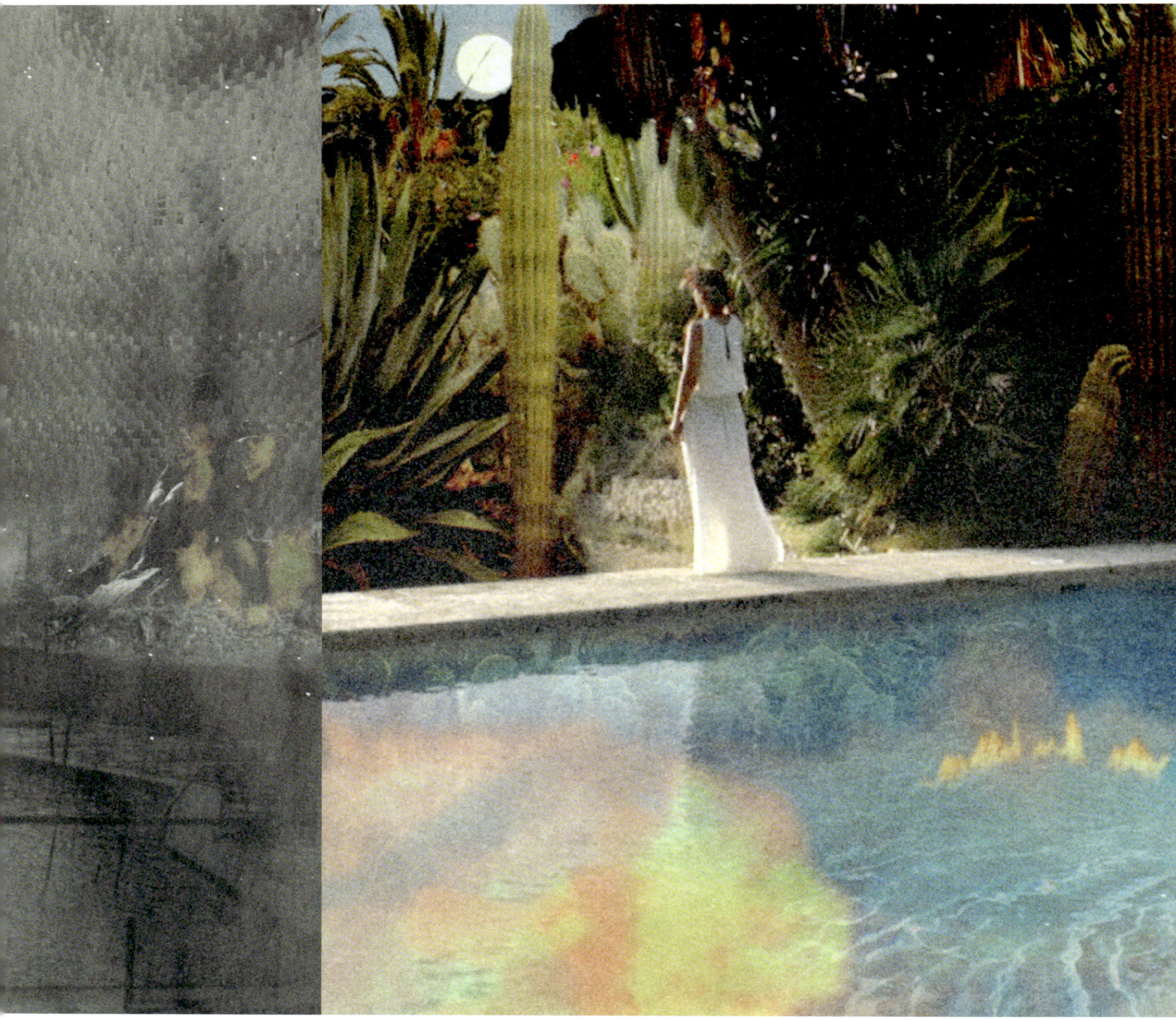

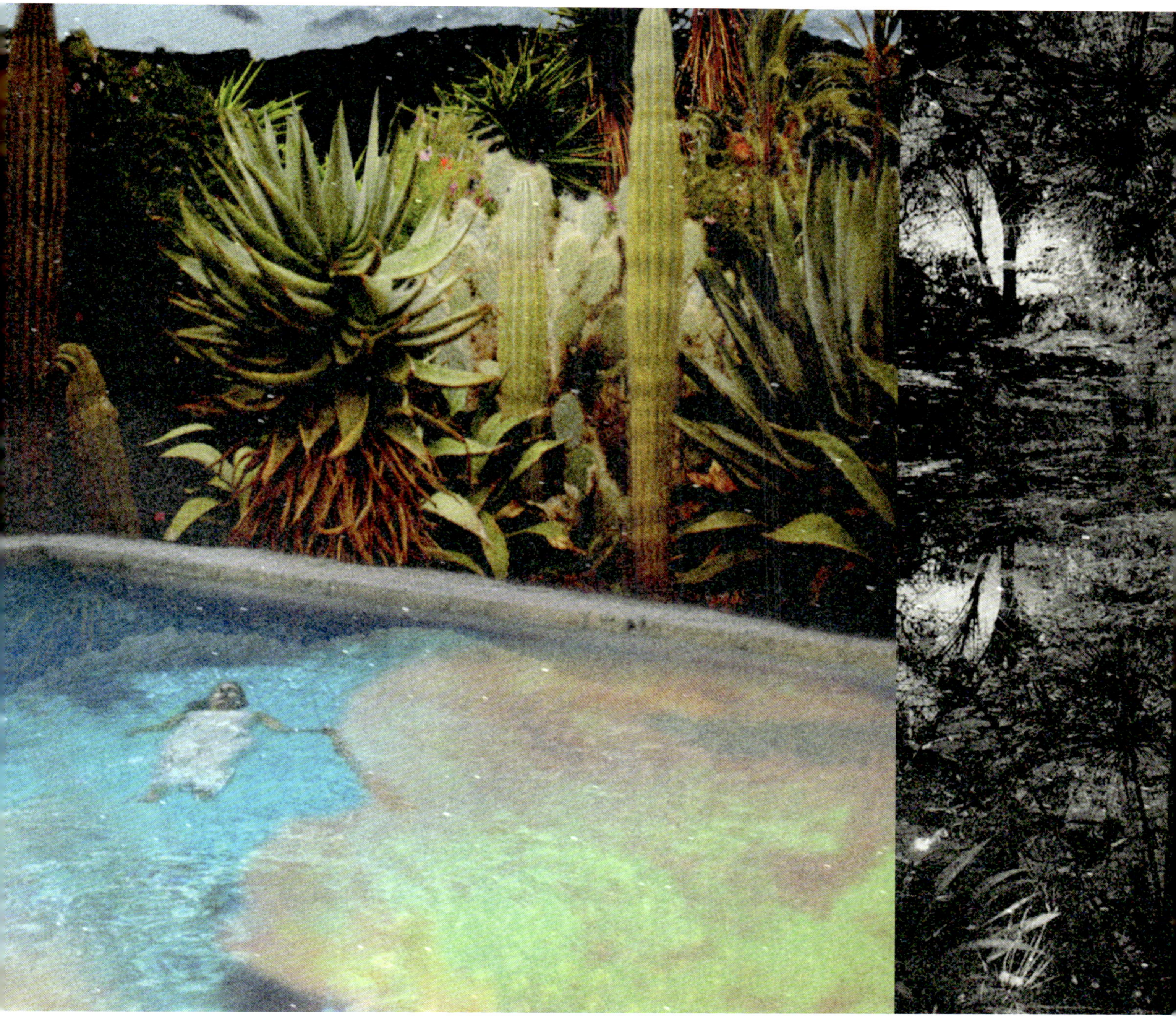

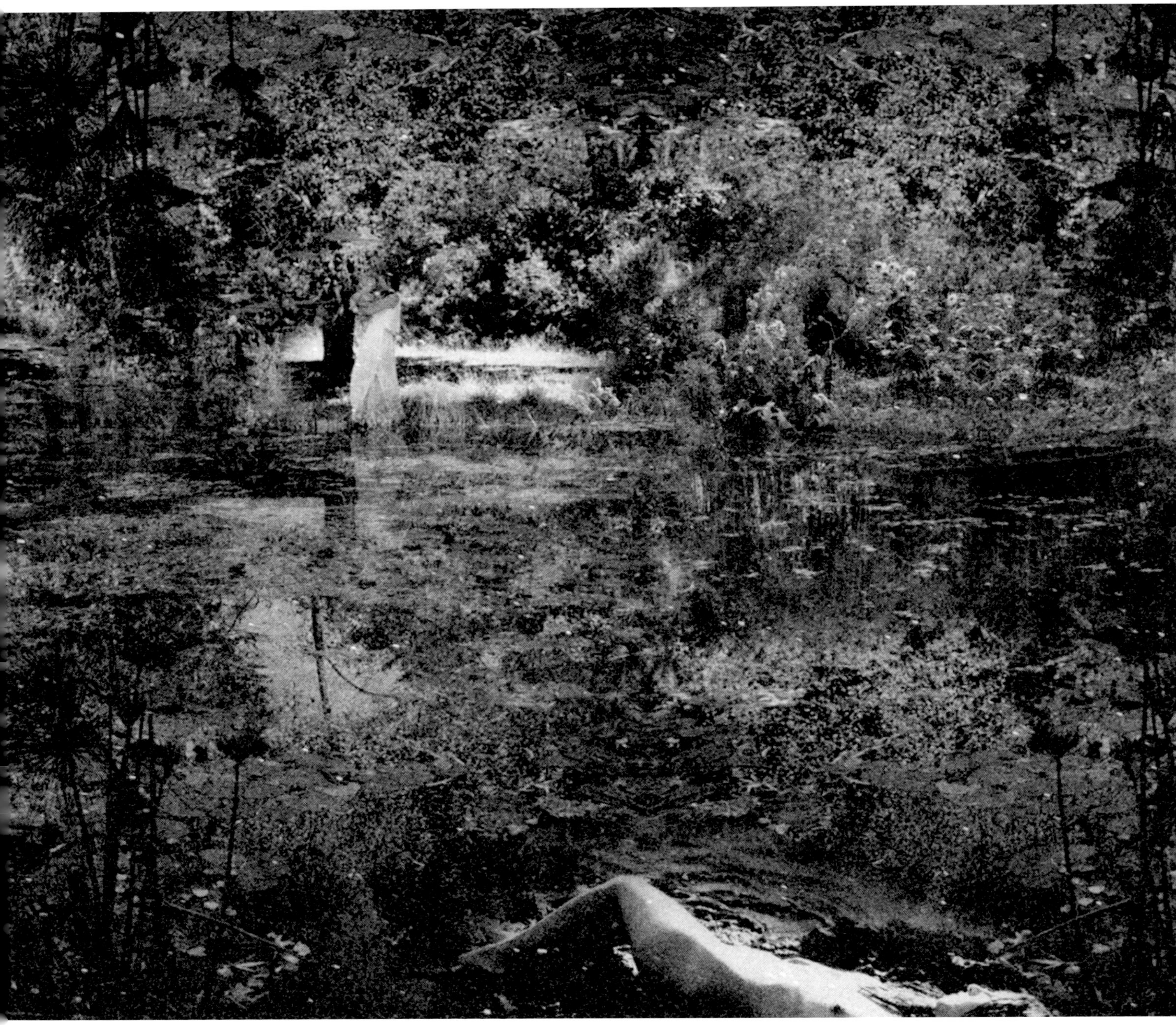

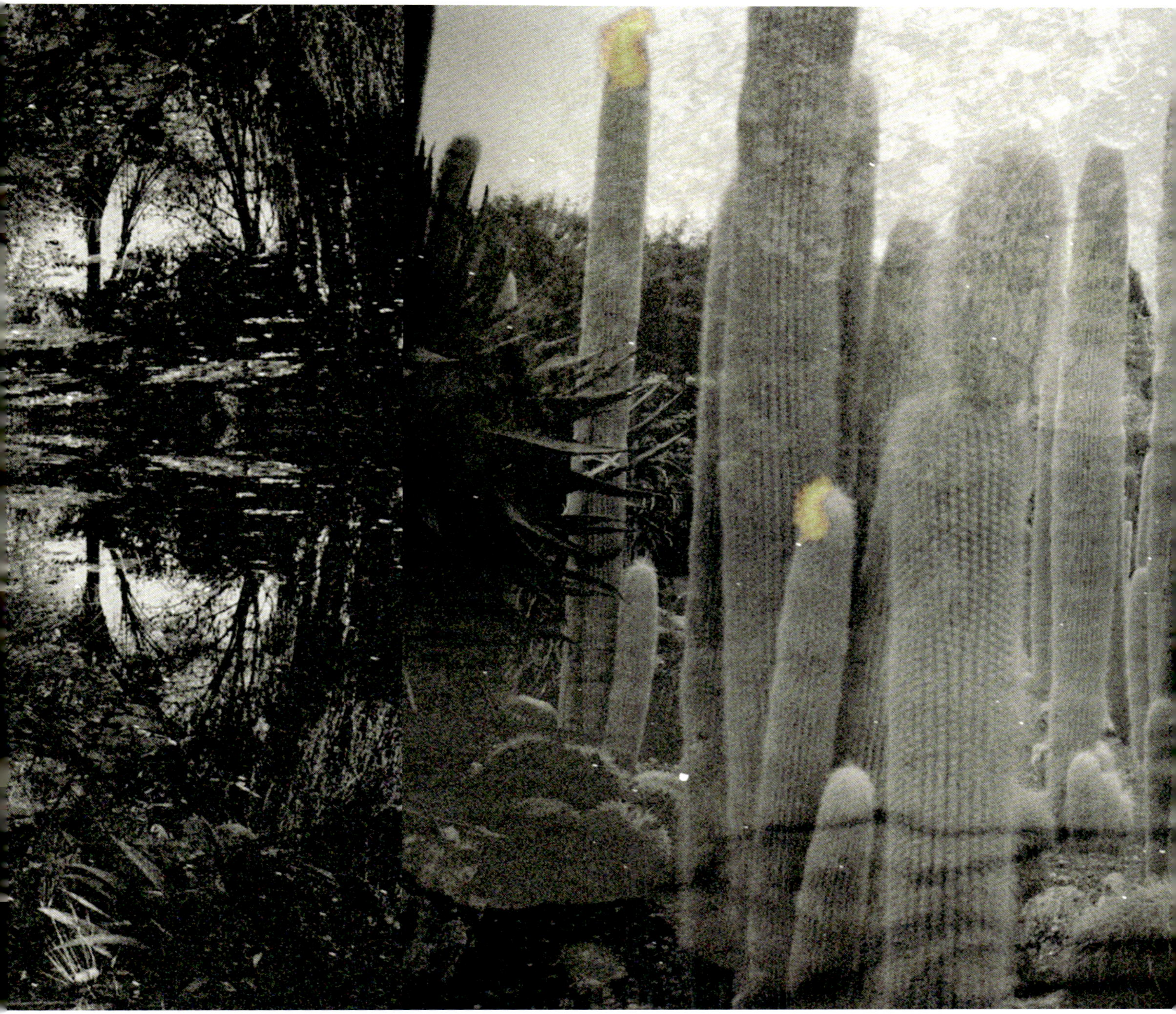

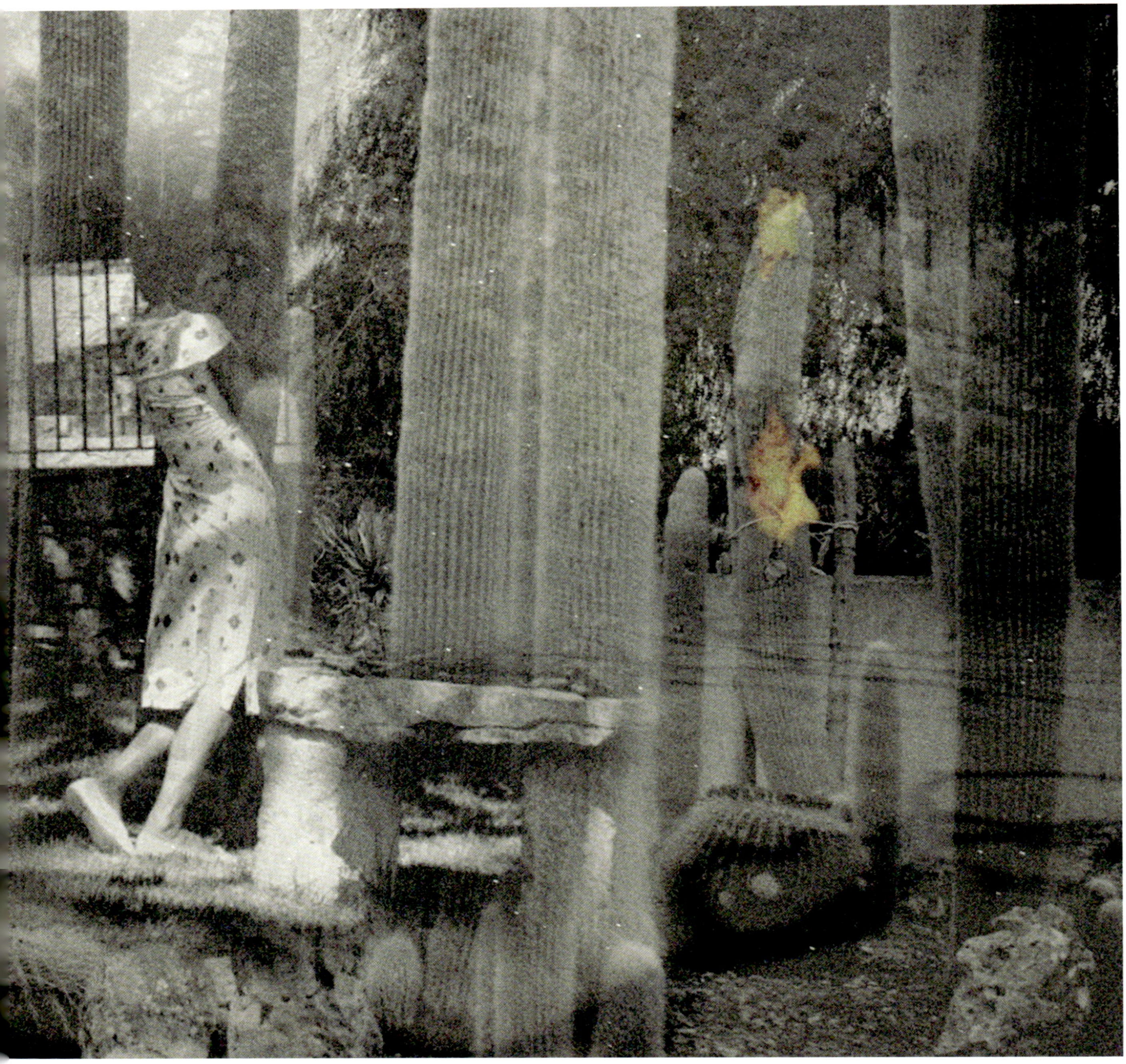

Anoir and the Woman in the Garden, Ciné Collage, 2015–2017

Reversing the Gaze
Refraction in the Mirror:
The Multidimensional Woman
The (Re)birth of HER_story

Ursula Maria Probst

The boundaries between reality and fiction in the current environment of accelerating information flow are porous – and imagination plays an increasingly important role. What if, instead of telling the story of the way our society fell out of an idyllic state, we asked how it came to be that we are trapped in such tight conceptual chains that we can no longer even imagine the possibility of reinventing ourselves?

Patricia Reinhart's work includes quotations from the psychoanalyst and social critic Arno Gruen. In his theory on the human struggle to survive, Gruen warns against a culture of non-being and the loss of interpersonal empathy. According to Gruen, thinking without empathy leads to an illusory world of abstractions, through which reality is no longer perceived directly and with due compassion.[1]

In her films, Patricia Reinhart critically examines processes of subjectification and practices of constructing and superimposing real inequalities and binary gender rules. Based on research-oriented practice from an artist's perspective while drawing from transdisciplinary literature, art history, film theory, psychology and sociology sources, she delves into the complexity of human behaviour with regard to gender-specific constructs. Female identity as an ongoing process of negotiation between self-image and images of others, between gender norms, role models and cultural ideas associated with femininity, is the engine that drives her cinematic work.

In a productive engagement with contemporary economies of image and gaze, Patricia Reinhart further develops cinematic techniques of the practice she calls "Ciné Collage" – inspired by Chris Marker's political science fiction *La Jetée* (1962), assembled from photographic stills. In her endtime scenario aesthetic, she produces films reminiscent of Andrei Tarkovsky and adapts visual methods of the projective Rorschach (inkblot) test used in psychodiagnostics for cinematic sequences that function as reflections, giving shape to the idea of manifestations as mirror images and critically reflecting on Jacques Lacan's theses on the formation of the subject – the mirror stage as formative of the function of the I. As Shoshana Felman[2] and Judith Butler[3] have discussed in fiercely debated feminist criticism, the Lacanian model of subjectification does not apply equally to both genders, for in Lacan's model the process is subject to the "primacy of the phallus", which always relegates the woman to the place of the Other. Judith Butler subsequently subjected the heteronormativity of Lacanian structural psychoanalysis to her own analysis and contrasts this with her concept of performativity of a psychoanalytic view of gender assumption. Patricia Reinhart's method of combining selected still images from her image archive creates a constant struggle between abstract patterns and figurative bodies or landscapes, of flora and fauna on the film surface, beyond a heteronormative determination of film towards its emancipatory potential as a speculative realm to bring us closer to new narratives.

Patricia Reinhart's filmmaking is a "One-Woman Production". She herself is author, actress, photographer, cinematographer, director, editor and, as a result of her use of complex film techniques – based on studies of silent film techniques, animated film and the Nouvelle Vague – we could add a "One-Woman Post-Production" to her skillset. She is involved in all film studio processes, in stagings by the pool, within landscapes, at the shore or in public spaces, seeing these as contributing to her integrity as an artist. While her beginnings were characterised by a playful spontaneity and an irrepressible desire to study character and articulate gestures and facial expressions of social, historical and literary female figures and roles – including the pose – as an intermediate zone between suggestion and attention, as an exemplary figure of transition, as an interweaving of self-dramatisation and imaging – to which she gives communicative weight in her films. Her current work is of an epic conceptuality. She combines the special effects of *Ciné Collage* she has been developing, whose technique she initially applied to stop-motion technique, then reconfigured for the present, with real staged actions, herself the protagonist, interweaving these features with salient details of places, historical settings, architectural and sculptural elements, whose hybrid fusion result in hitherto unseen film sequences of a compelling, animated and virtual world.

In her early productions, Patricia Reinhart shows how various systems, actions and emotions can overlap, how gestures and feelings are integrated into relationships. She develops techniques that allow her figures (mainly embodied by herself as she enters the scene in multiple roles) to interact. In her search for interfaces between individual life and the cultural memory of humanity, in particular the situation of women, Patricia Reinhart employs a decidedly vigilant, poetic and political use of the medium of film and its technical innovations.

Ciné Collage is thus the designation for a layering technique that transfers collage-making methods to film, as it were, creating a metafictional mirroring of scenes through the montage of images. When Patricia Reinhart uses different sources and shifts meaning poetically through *Ciné Collage*, new visual forms emerge that collide with cinematic conventions. As a painter who works in layers she transfers her self conception to the medium of film, thereby gaining depth of colour and form. In addition to her painting practice, she derives her cinematographic vocabulary from her considerable acting skills; parallel to her painting studies, she studied acting. To avoid copyright conflicts, she decided early on to use her own material, her own still images and video recordings. In the meantime, she has an extensive archive of up to 500 photos per theme. She repeatedly photographs single frames to break the illusion of continuity of the finished film, which consists of montages of frozen, still images that recall the stillness of the filmstrip, a kind of necrosis that underlines the incredible vitality of her films.

With a keen eye, Patricia Reinhart analyses inequalities that manifest themselves in real life and are reflected in literature, film and art, appealing to emancipatory processes as she herself performs, slipping into countless female roles as she embodies historical and literary female figures such as Shakespeare's Ophelia or Dreyer's Joan of Arc, posing questions of female identity in specific social contexts or using them as metaphors for understanding social phenomena. After examining silent movies, their techniques in creating pictorial illusions, and animated film, Patricia Reinhart became intensively involved with Nouvelle Vague, especially Jean-Luc Godard and the female characters portrayed by Anna Karina, in particular in *Vivre sa vie* (1962), *Alphaville* (1965) and *Pierrot le fou* (1965). "This particular film aesthetic of the 1960s brought me to my self-portraits, which are made exclusively in the Paris Photomatons", says Patricia Reinhart, bridging a connection to her photographic work. "In addition, I studied the *Untitled Film Stills* by Cindy Sherman [from the years 1977 to 1980], which subsequently inspired me to create my own film sequences."[4]

Images not only (re)produce the visible, but also suggest dominant norms and normalities. The feminist film theorist Kaja Silverman's analysis of the gaze regimes that determine what appears on the screen in the cultural image repertoire provides a clue about the parameters of representation, how to deal with being mirrored and how to resist appropriation by such reflected images. From a representation-critical point of view, Patricia Reinhart develops procedures for arriving at other images, images which, through her techniques, occupy a productive distance from what has been seen before. Like the reinventor of cinema forms Chantal Akerman, Patricia Reinhart develops her own dramaturgy from a feminist point of view as she transgresses genre boundaries with a pronounced sense of durability and experience across time.

The following three works are taken from an apocalyptic film cycle that Patricia Reinhart started over 10 years ago in order to portray a possible end-of-the-world scenario. This series also includes films such as: *Die ihr Brot mit Tränen aß (Requiem for an Unendurable Paradise)* (2013/2014) and *Kirkirerland* (2008). The question is addressed: How can one cope with certain death; how does one behave at the end of the world? Partly it is acceptance, partly it is a struggle for survival or a hopelessness in search of a different future that we encounter in the films. This is made visible both in the complex iconography of the images and in the use of special cinematographic techniques.

Anoir and the Woman in the Garden (2015–2017) is one of the major works in Patricia Reinhart's cinematic œuvre – a film of great epic power, which explores the beauty of ethical political values (embodied by a woman in a white dress), the power ego (represented by a peacock), apocalyptic doom (visualised by an explosive inferno of terror) and attempted solutions after the end of the world in the form of a naked woman emerging from the sea. She represents the

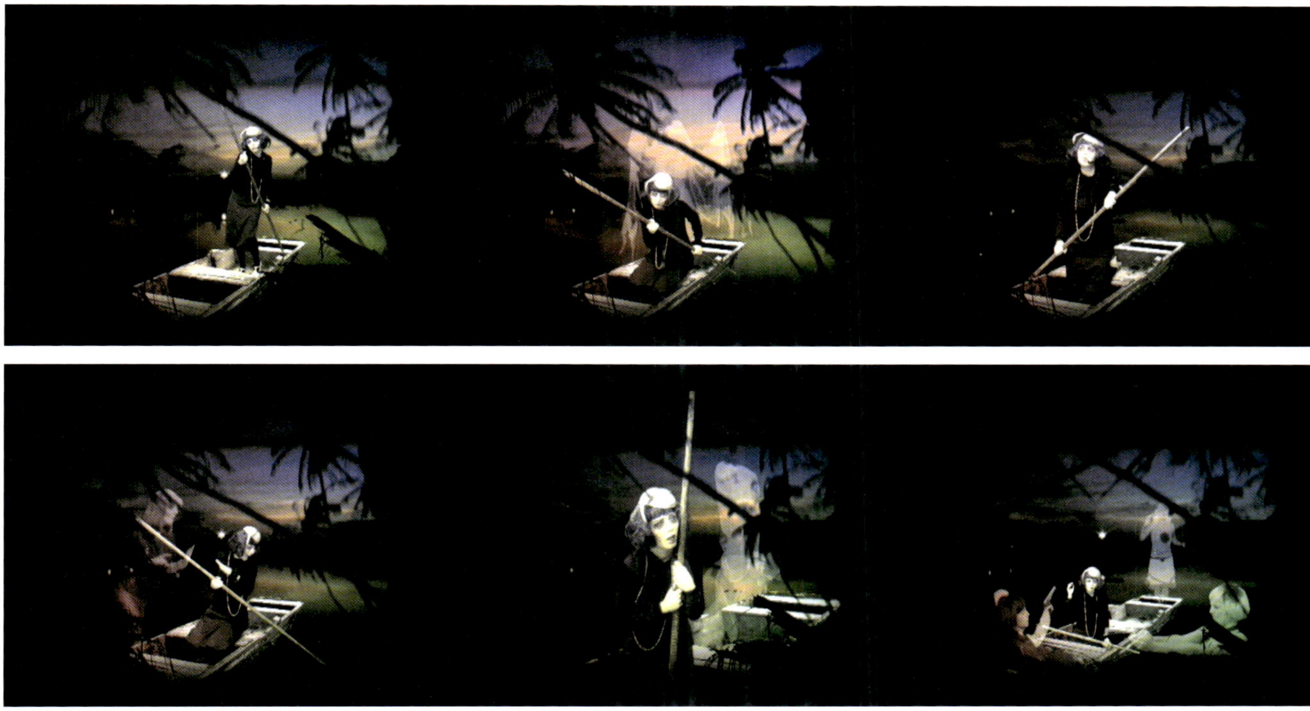

Kirkirerland, Ciné Collage, 2008

drawn image of a version of the future. Cross-references to Greek mythology, in which Europa, daughter of King Agenor, was abducted by Zeus, who was transformed into a bull, outline the transition from a patriarchal to a matriarchal order. Images of statues depicting those women as warriors, a female figure referencing the painter Frida Kahlo in a labyrinthine garden of phallus-like burning cacti (image of the female artist rebelling in a patriarchal system) or in front of a bay with a mirror in her hand next to lilies symbolic of fertility, scenes of a mother with a baby in the middle of a garden of paradise (the filming/location material originates from Monet's garden in Giverny), in whose scene a hell reflected in a mirror crystallises, are stretched into dense image and sound sequences. Patricia Reinhart's extraordinary ability to stage dramaturgically reference-rich content in an almost operatic manner with visual opulence is borne by a passion for working with complex arrangements of image composition even in risky locations (filming took place on the cliffs near Marseille and on Mallorca). Patricia Reinhart uses the landscape space as a stage and incorporates the unpredictability of nature into a backdrop for her choreography. "Max Ernst's collages from *Une semaine de bonté* [from 1943] showed me possibilities to create new stages of an apocalyptic world."[5] Seawater becomes the symbol of a struggle for survival between death, redemption and rebirth. *Anoir and the Woman in the Garden* is an artistic short film whose iconographic density reveals contours of a reflective theory of morality. As a moral authority and last survivor after the end of the world, a nun appearing in the rocky landscape initially represents goodness and faith in the world. Enigmatically inspired as a female counterpart by *Der Mönch am Meer* (1808–1810) by Caspar David Friedrich, she gazes at the sea, radiating a radical loneliness. But even she has lost faith in the face of a man-made inferno. What follows is her suicide. How is this apparent contrast between arriving in a "post-moral" time and the simultaneous recognition of the indispensability of applied ethics to be understood? Parallels exist with Pier Paolo Pasolini's film *Il Vangelo secondo Matteo* (1964) in the uncompromising manner with which the political and religious establishment is engaged. *Anoir and the Woman in the Garden* is composed as a visual piece of music and rhythmically intercut with the electronic soundscape of Frédéric D. Oberland, whose original sound Patricia Reinhart altered through lengthened distortions, creating another dimension to captivate the senses through the temporal transfer and acoustic mirror thus manifested. Through the interplay of performance, film and sound techniques, the film as organism gains magical intensity.

Patricia Reinhart's own body as a performative agent refers not only to what is human and alive in a biological sense – and therefore also mortal – but to historical as well as contemporary manifestations of an ever-increasing complexity of agency. To make new narratives imaginable and create space for an interconnected, complicated and complex reality, Patricia Reinhart uses the metaphor of death. She seems driven to always be one step ahead.

The work *13 Poèmes visibles (Ophélia & Avant de mourir)* (2011) shows how film analysis and cinematic production

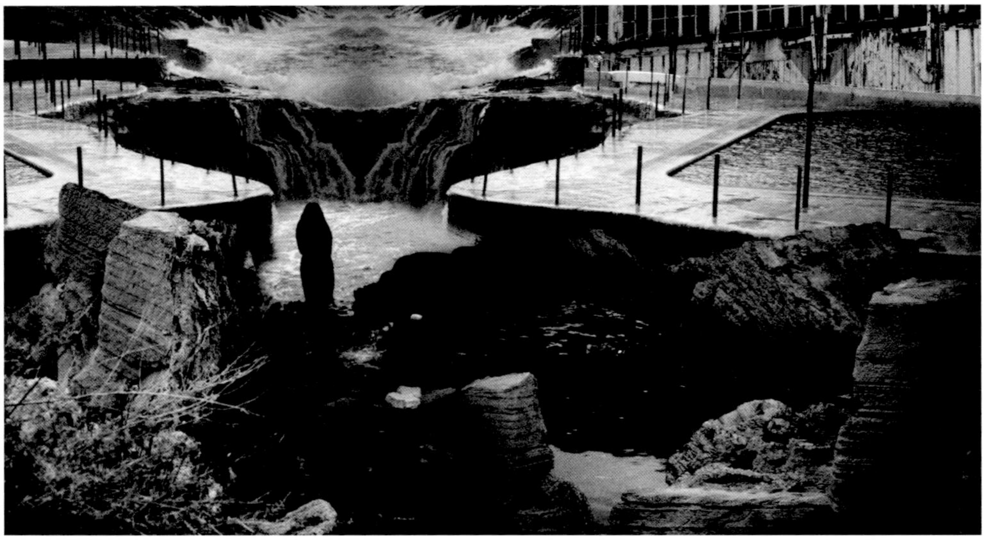

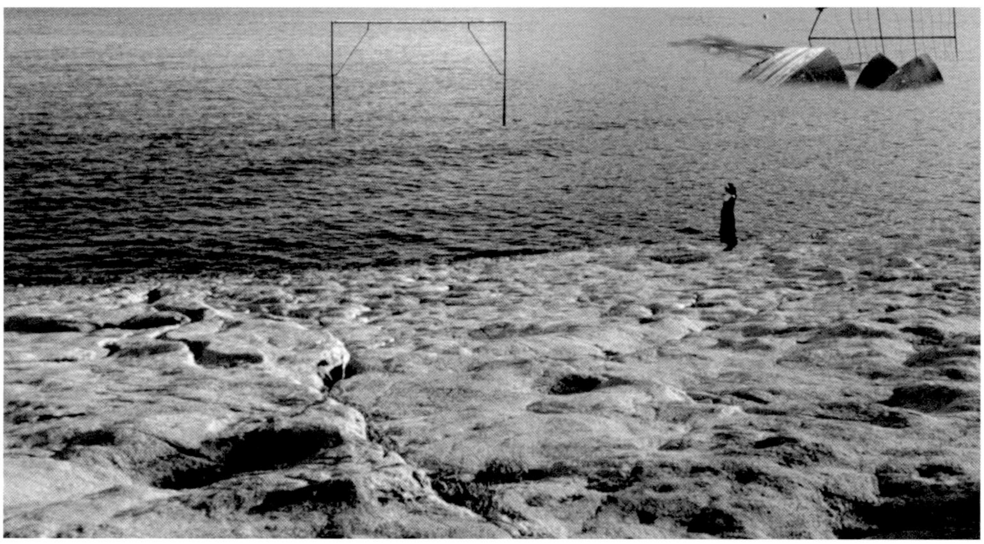

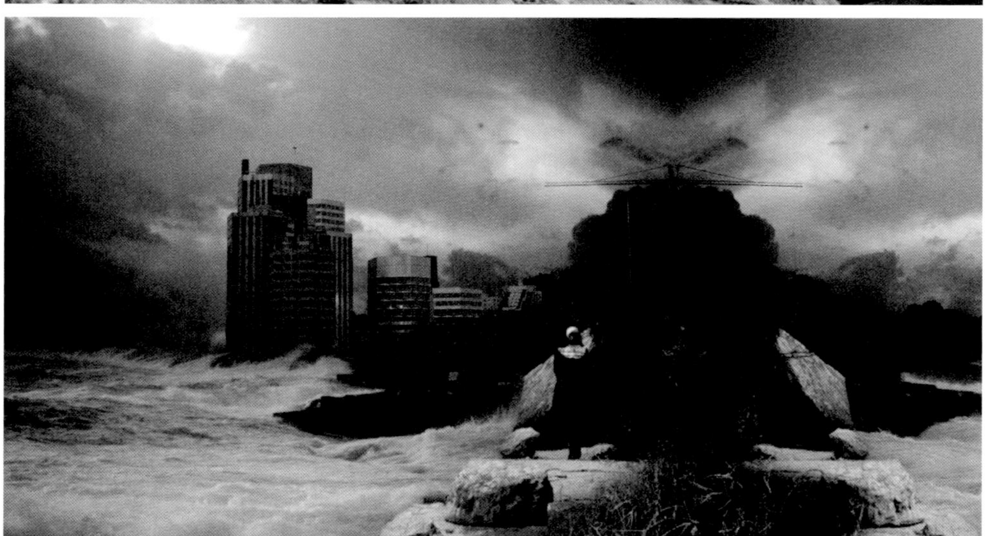

Anoir and the Woman in the Garden, Ciné Collage, 2015–2017

techniques are synergistic. In the original, the thirteen Super-8 films run in parallel in 8–35 second loops as a spatial installation, forming a nearly orchestral arrangement. The underlying concept of this symphonic encounter of thirteen portraits of women is inspired by the publication *Speaking about Godard*[6], based on conversations between the feminist film theorist Kaja Silverman – via post-structuralism and psychoanalysis – and the avant-garde filmmaker Harun Farocki about Godard's most important films and their formal and theoretical innovations. In the chapter *Nana is an animal,* Godard's film *Vivre sa vie* is referenced in a reading as they discuss each scene in detail. Patricia Reinhart ties in with their film analyses: "This conversation led me to the images and functioned as a tool of sorts, so that I saw in it a new order for me that provided me with a structure to give my ideas a conceptual 'corset of form' which I needed for the *Poèmes*."[7] In the analogue experimentation with Super-8 film material and in the conscious use of the fragile medium of film (tear, burn-through, wear), evidence of use is employed as an aesthetic form to represent the drama of actual human fragility.

Patricia Reinhart uses historical, literary and cinematic references to trace a clear path to the present. Her scene featuring Joan of Arc refers to the 1928 historical film *La Passion de Jeanne d'Arc* by Carl Theodor Dreyer. In 1962, Jean-Luc Godard made his fourth feature film *Vivre sa vie: film en douze tableaux,* an essayistic, documentary account of the everyday life of the young prostitute Nana, in which his wife at the time, Anna Karina, played the leading role. About 14 minutes into the film, we see Nana sitting in a cinema watching a particularly pointed, transcendental scene from Carl Theodor Dreyer's masterpiece starring Maria Falconetti. It shows Joan of Arc waiting to die. Patricia Reinhart refers to these scenes from Godard's film and Dreyer's masterpiece. She is interested in the drama of this female figure who, although she does everything right in the male world in which she engaged and helped France to victory, was accused of heresy, condemned to death and executed. This image of a woman who died unjustly and at the same time accepted it herself in the face of her religious upbringing forms one of a total of thirteen sequences inspired in their staging by silent film stars such as Asta Nielsen, Lyda Borelli or Pola Negri. Extravagant women in the limelight who were considered divas and revered as "divinities" and whose self-confident ambitions for self-empowerment often ended dramatically with an untimely death. The subtexts written for them deal with death, redemption and confrontation with others – referencing Virginia Woolf's *A Room of One's Own* (1929)[8] in the process – raise questions as to how perspectives on freedom, personal responsibility and visions emerge, address violence and influence victim and perpetrator roles, male and/or female. We meet self-determined women who fail due to external circumstances. A short sequence of 13 seconds shows a woman being shot and blood flowing from her upper body. "Aren't all dreams and visions immediately destroyed within this system?",[9] asks Patricia Reinhart. From what entanglements is it necessary to free oneself? Why are historical operas and plays still performed in versions in which the heroines are often doomed to die? The character of Ophelia, which she stages on film, refers to a painting by John Everett Millais (1852) and to Shakespeare's Ophelia in *Hamlet* (around 1600–1602), which is one of William Shakespeare's most controversial works to date. Various adaptations exist in which Ophelia and Hamlet's love affair is being questioned. Asta Nielsen took on the title role in 1921 and was the first actress to play a woman disguised as a man, altering Hamlet's gender. "This film with Asta Nielsen led me to the characters – especially her own strange interpretation of the theatrical transposition, in particular her stiff arm movements from top to bottom in one scene",[10] Patricia Reinhart explains, pointing to her intensive study of the silent movie stars, whose careers ended abruptly with the switch to talking movies.

Patricia Reinhart focuses on two aspects at the same time: on the one hand, her authenticity as an artist, and on the other, prevailing social conditions for women, spanning these into a cultural-historical genealogy. The contradiction between the precariousness of her protagonists and the desire for an opulence of images is striking. This contradictory conundrum can be compared with Michel Foucault's concept of heterotopia, with the help of which she establishes a relationship between the utopian, imaginary dimensions of her real, unrelated images and their material, tangible dimensions. Heterotopia can be seen in the context of Patricia Reinhart's *Ciné Collages* applied to the three-channel video installation *Ein Nachtstück* (2011/2012) as a visualisation of imaginary places and parallel worlds that create space for new experiential horizons. The *Ciné Collage* as heterotopia creates an illusion of apparent (nightmarish) dreaminess. "In *Ein Nachtstück* a female figure appears in Peter Doig's canoe",[11] says Patricia Reinhart, lending insight into existing references woven into her film sequences like subtle quotations. These strands act as threads that intertwine. Shot in Paris, Patricia Reinhart's visualisation shows how the past survives in the form of an "historical present" in architecture, demonstrating the way in which past and present occur simultaneously.

The act of perception becomes a revelation, a moment of difference. I know that what I am looking at is not real, yet it brings me closer to reality. Patricia Reinhart's artistic independence consists in also being critical of the techniques she uses and in confronting them with fantasies of feasibility. In the process of cinematic elaboration, she is indeed a visual eccentric, working without a script, using sketches to visually maximise her films, in which still images and video

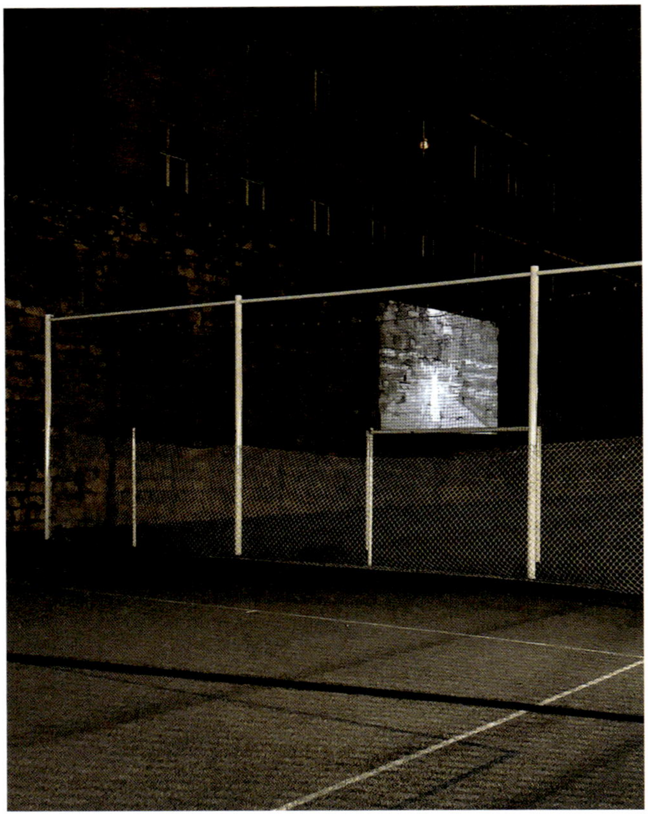

Installation view / Installationsansicht / Vue de l'installation
Nuit Blanche, Paris, 2018
Anoir and the Woman in the Garden, Ciné Collage, 2015–2017

sequences join together like elementary particles even as categorical demarcations dissolve. Her explosive visual creativity will give rise to essayistic treatises of an unpredictable work and a sceptical attitude towards the modern belief that reality can be grasped through image constructions.

In her early short films, Patricia Reinhart stages humorous portraits, everyday scenes and slapstick imbued with the charm of the silent film era. She has mastered the art of transformation. With her acting talent and a reliable comedic sensibility, beautiful grimaces hark back to the early days of film in self-made miniature sets with simple props. She uses the media practices that photography and film have in common, namely focusing from a certain point of view to stage and manipulate through framing and the options of self-reflection of one's own media process. Her research on the filmmaker Maya Deren, on her experimental films from the 1940s and their development of the specific art form of video dance, is followed by an intensive examination of Maya Deren's film theories and a cinematic manner of thinking that opens up intersensory worlds. As in Maya Deren's films, Patricia Reinhart's cinematic œuvre includes creative action in generous amounts, gaining gravitas through the manipulation of time and space, both in pre- and post-production.

Patricia Reinhart operates the camera using a tripod and self-timer; the intimate moment (of being completely alone), the search for the authentic image of being, is essential during the shoot and the staging in public spaces. In the studio, she arranges photo sequences in the manner of *Ciné Collage*, which enables her to enter the picture herself several times in a kaleidoscope-like manner and to resist a hegemonic visual dispositive, displaying a feminist impetus in altering the rules of the gaze, relations of dominance, conventions of perception and visualisation. Following the film theorist Kaja Silverman, the concept of the gaze regime can also be used to grasp the (re)effect of perceptual structures on the constitution of the subject and thus on gender; in this respect, this insistent confrontation with conventional gaze norms can be seen as a cultural practice. Poetic image sequences emerge from post-dramatic aesthetics developed in this way, which become film through montage – at a crossroads between performance, art and film history.

What's next? Perhaps we need to ask ourselves how much our current art and literary practice gives nourishment to new realisms that maintain a relationship to reality. We need to ask ourselves how the distance between the possible and the real might be bridged. In her films Patricia Reinhart resembles a novelist by shaping her characters who courageously follow a passion, the self-referential potential of which intensifies and at the same time subversively undermines gaze regimes.

Ursula Maria Probst is an art historian, art critic, artist and freelance curator for Fluc, KÖR, Public Art Niederösterreich, freiraum MQ. 2019–2022 Curator for the Artist-in-Residence program *Body Embedding* Austria/Southeast Asia. 2013–2019 Billboard project *Transcultural Emancipation*, KulturKontakt Austria / BKA / Fluc. 2016–2019 FLUCA Austrian Cultural Pavilion, Plovdiv, Bulgaria. 2016 Curator-in-Residence in Rio de Janeiro. 2015 Curator of the Austrian contributions for the Havana Biennial. Lectures and projects in Myanmar, Slovenia, Vietnam, Ukraine, Russia, China, Cyprus, etc.

1 Arno Gruen, *The Betrayal of the Self: The Fear of Autonomy in Men and Women* (1986), New York 1988.
2 Shoshana Felman, *The Literary Speech Act. Don Juan with J. L. Austin, or Seduction in Two Languages*, Ithaca, NY 1983.
3 Judith Butler, *Gender Trouble. Feminism and the Subversion of Identity*, New York 1990.
4 Patricia Reinhart in conversation in November 2021.
5 Ibid.
6 Kaja Silverman, Harun Farocki, *Speaking about Godard*, New York 1998.
7 Patricia Reinhart in conversation in November 2021.
8 Virginia Woolf, *A Room of One's Own*, London 1929.
9 Patricia Reinhart in conversation in November 2021.
10 Ibid.
11 Ibid.

Wie versuchen, es umzukehren? Brechung im Spiegel: Die mehrdimensionale Frau The (Re)birth of HER_story

Ursula Maria Probst

Die gegenwärtige Welt der sich beschleunigenden Informationsströme weist poröse Grenzen zwischen Realität und Fiktion auf. Das Imaginäre spielt darin eine zunehmend größere Rolle. Was wäre, wenn wir, anstatt die Geschichte zu erzählen, wie unsere Gesellschaft aus einem idyllischen Zustand herausgefallen ist, fragen würden, wie es dazu kam, dass wir in so engen konzeptionellen Fesseln gefangen sind, dass für uns nicht einmal mehr vorstellbar ist, uns neu zu erfinden?

In Texten über Patricia Reinharts Werk sind Zitate des Psychoanalytikers und Gesellschaftskritikers Arno Gruen zu finden, der in seiner Theorie zum menschlichen Überlebenskampf vor einer Kultur des Nichtseins und vor dem Verlust der zwischenmenschlichen Empathie warnt. Laut Gruen führt Denken ohne Empathie zu einer Scheinwelt aus Abstraktionen, durch welche die Wirklichkeit nicht mehr unmittelbar und mitfühlend wahrgenommen wird.[1]

Patricia Reinhart nimmt in ihren Filmen Prozesse der Subjektivierung sowie Praktiken der Konstruktion und Überlagerung realer Ungleichheiten und binärer Geschlechterordnungen kritisch unter die Lupe. Ausgehend von einer Artist-Research-orientierten Praxis, die transdisziplinär Quellen aus Literatur, Kunstgeschichte, Filmtheorie, Psychologie und Soziologie heranzieht, betreibt sie intensive Forschungen zur Komplexität menschlichen Verhaltens unter genderspezifischen Vorzeichen. Weibliche Identität als andauernder Ausverhandlungsprozess zwischen Selbst- und Fremdbildern, zwischen Geschlechternormen, Leitbildern und den mit Weiblichkeit verbundenen kulturellen Vorstellungen sind die Reibungsfläche für ihr filmisches Schaffen.

In produktiver Auseinandersetzung mit gegenwärtigen Bild- und Blickökonomien entwickelt Patricia Reinhart filmische Techniken der von ihr als „Ciné Collage" bezeichneten Praktik – inspiriert durch Chris Markers politischen Science-Fiction-Film *La Jetée* (1962), der aus fotografischen Standbildern montiert ist – weiter. Sie produziert in ihrer Endzeitszenarien-Ästhetik an Andrei Tarkowski erinnernde Filme und adaptiert visuelle Methoden des in der Psychodiagnostik eingesetzten projektiven Rorschach-Tests (Tintenkleckstest) für filmische Sequenzen, die als Spiegelungen fungieren sowie der Vorstellung von Bildern als Spiegelbild Gestalt geben und Jacques Lacans Thesen der Subjektwerdung – das Spiegelstadium als Bildner der Ichfunktion – kritisch reflektieren. Wie in der feministischen Kritik durch Shoshana Felman[2] und Judith Butler[3] heftig diskutiert wurde, gilt das lacansche Modell der Subjektivierungsprozesse nicht in gleicher Weise für beide Geschlechter, denn der Prozess unterliegt bei Lacan dem „Primat des Phallus", der die Frau immer an den Ort des Anderen verweist. Judith Butler unterzog in Folge die Heteronormativität der strukturalen Psychoanalyse lacanscher Prägung einer Untersuchung und stellte dieser ihr Konzept der Performativität der psychoanalytischen Auffassung von der Annahme des Geschlechts gegenüber. Patricia Reinharts Methode der Kombination ausgewählter Standbilder aus ihrem Bildarchiv erzeugt ein ständiges Ringen zwischen abstrakten Mustern und figurativen Körpern oder Landschaften, von Flora und Fauna auf der Filmoberfläche – weg von einer heteronormativen Bestimmung des Films, hin zu einem emanzipatorischen Potenzial und damit zu einem spekulativen Bereich, um uns neue Narrative näherzubringen.

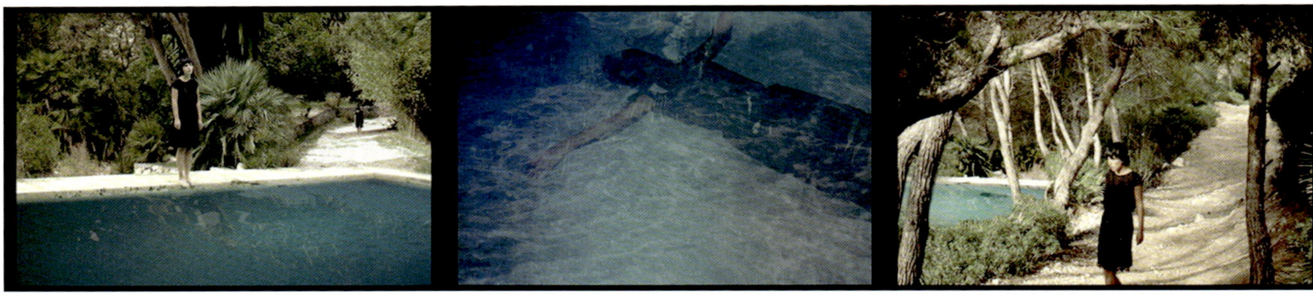

Die ihr Brot mit Tränen aß (Requiem for an Unendurable Paradise), Ciné Collage, 2013/14

Patricia Reinharts Filmschaffen ist eine „One-Woman Production". Sie selbst ist Autorin, Akteurin, Fotografin, Kamerafrau, Regisseurin, Cutterin, und angesichts der Anwendung komplexer filmtechnischer Verfahren – die auf Studien zu Techniken des Stummfilms, des Trickfilms und der Nouvelle Vague basieren – könnten wir hinzufügen, dass sie des Weiteren eine „One-Woman Post-Production" ist. In jeden der Abläufe im Filmstudio oder jede der Inszenierungen am Pool, in Landschaften, am Meer oder im öffentlichen Raum ist sie selbst involviert; sie sieht darin ein wichtiges Kriterium ihrer künstlerischen Authentizität. Sind ihre Anfänge von einer spielerischen Spontaneität und durch eine unbändige Lust am Charakterstudium und an der Artikulation der Gestik und Mimik sozialer, historischer und literarischer Frauenfiguren und -rollen sowie an der Pose – als Zwischenzone zwischen Suggestion und Pointierung, als exemplarische Figur des Übergangs, als Verschränkung von Selbstinszenierung und Bildgebung – charakterisiert, denen sie in ihren Filmen einen sprechenden Körper gibt, so ist ihr aktuelles Werk von einer epischen Konzeptualität. Die von ihr entwickelten Spezialeffekte der *Ciné Collage*, deren Technik sie zunächst ausgehend von der Stop-Motion-Technik anwendet und für die Gegenwart neu konfiguriert, kombiniert sie mit real inszenierten Handlungen, in denen sie selbst die Protagonistin ist. Hinzu kommt eine Verschränkung mit verschiedenen Details von Orten, historischen Schauplätzen, architektonischen und skulpturalen Elementen, aus deren Kombination und hybrider Fusion bis dato nicht gesehene Filmsequenzen einer animierten, virtuellen Welt resultieren.

Bereits in den Anfängen zeigt Patricia Reinhart in ihren Videos, wie sich verschiedene Systeme, Handlungen, Emotionen überlagern können, wie Gesten und Regungen in Beziehungen eingebunden sind. Sie entwickelt Techniken, die ihre Figuren (vorwiegend von ihr selbst, multipel ins Bild tretend, verkörpert) interagieren lassen. Auf der Suche nach Schnittstellen zwischen individuellem Leben und dem Menschheitsgedächtnis, im Speziellen zur Situation der Frau, verfolgt Patricia Reinhart einen wachsamen, poetischen und politischen Gebrauch des Mediums Film und dessen technischer Neuerungen.

Ciné Collage liefert das Stichwort für eine in Schichten funktionierende Technik, die Methoden der Collage auf den Film überträgt und durch die Bildmontage eine metafiktionale Reflexion der Szenen bewirkt. Neue visuelle Formen entstehen, die mit filmischen Konventionen die Klinge kreuzen, indem sich Patricia Reinhart verschiedener Quellen bedient und durch die *Ciné Collage* poetische Bedeutungsverschiebungen vornimmt. Ihr Selbstverständnis, als Malerin in Schichten zu arbeiten, überträgt sie auf das Medium Film, wodurch Tiefe in der Farb- und Formgebung gewonnen wird. Ihr kinematografisches Vokabular leitet sie nicht nur aus ihrer malerischen Praxis, sondern auch von ihren schauspielerischen Fähigkeiten ab – parallel zu ihrem Studium der Malerei machte sie eine Schauspielausbildung. Um Konflikte über Urheberrechtsansprüche zu vermeiden, entschied sie sich bereits in den Anfängen, eigenes Material, eigene Standbilder und Videoshoots zu verwenden. Mittlerweile verfügt sie über ein umfassendes Archiv mit bis zu 500 Fotos pro Motiv. Sie fotografiert immer wieder Einzelbilder, um die Illusion der Kontinuität des Films, der aus der Montage von Standbildern resultiert, in gefrierenden Augenblicken zu brechen – erinnernd an die Stille des Filmstreifens, an jene Nekrose, welche die unglaubliche Vitalität ihrer Filme unterstreicht.

Mit geschärftem Blick analysiert Patricia Reinhart filmisch sich im realen Leben manifestierende und in Literatur, Film und Kunst widerspiegelnde Ungleichbehandlungen, appelliert an emanzipatorische Prozesse und performt, indem sie selbst in unzählige Frauenrollen schlüpft oder historische und literarische Frauenfiguren wie Shakespeares Ophelia oder Dreyers Jeanne d'Arc verkörpert, Fragen weiblicher Identität in spezifischen gesellschaftlichen Kontexten stellt oder sie als Metapher für gesellschaftliche Phänomene heranzieht. Nach einer Auseinandersetzung mit dem Stummfilm und dessen Techniken in der Erzeugung von Bildillusionen sowie mit dem Trickfilm befasste sich Patricia Reinhart intensiv mit der Nouvelle Vague, vor allem mit Jean-Luc Godard und den Frauenfiguren, die von Anna Karina dargestellt wurden, im Speziellen in *Vivre sa vie* (1962), *Alphaville* (1965) und *Pierrot le fou* (1965). „Diese Filmästhetik der 1960er-Jahre brachte mich zu meinen Selbstporträts, die ausschließlich in den Pariser Photomatons angefertigt werden", spannt Patricia Reinhart den Bogen zu ihrem fotografischen Werk. „Außerdem [waren es] die *Untitled Film Stills* von Cindy Sherman [aus den Jahren 1977 bis 1980], die mich in weiterer Folge auch zu meinen Filmsequenzen führten."[4]

Bilder (re)produzieren nicht nur das Sichtbare, sondern auch dominierende Normen und Normalitäten. Die feministische Filmtheoretikerin Kaja Silverman liefert durch ihre Analyse der Blickregimes, durch die bestimmt wird, was im kulturellen Bildrepertoire auf dem Bildschirm (= Screen) erscheint, einen Anhaltspunkt für Darstellungsparameter, wie mit dem Gespiegeltwerden umgegangen werden kann und wie es gelingt, sich einer Vereinnahmung seitens der Bilder zu widersetzen. Aus einer repräsentationskritischen Sicht entwickelt Patricia Reinhart Verfahren, um zu anderen Bildern zu gelangen, zu Bildern, die durch die von ihr angewandten Techniken gegenüber dem Vor-Gesehenen eine produktive Distanz einnehmen. Wie die Neuerfinderin der Formen des Kinos Chantal Akerman entwickelt Patricia Reinhart aus einer feministischen Sichtweise eine eigene Dramaturgie im Überschreiten von Genregrenzen mit einem ausgeprägten Sinn für Dauer und Zeiterfahrung.

Die folgenden drei beschriebenen Werke sind einem apokalyptischen Filmzyklus entsprungen, mit dem Patricia Reinhart vor über zehn Jahren begann, um ein mögliches Ende der Welt zu zeichnen. Zu dieser Serie zählen zudem Filme wie *Die ihr Brot mit Tränen aß (Requiem for an Unendurable Paradise)* (2013/14) und *Kirkirerland* (2008). Im Mittelpunkt steht eine zentrale Frage: Wie wird mit dem sicheren Tod umgegangen; wie verhält man/frau sich am Ende der Welt? Teilweise ist es Akzeptanz, teilweise ist es ein Überlebenskampf oder eine Hoffnungslosigkeit auf der Suche nach einer anderen Zukunft, auf die wir in den Filmen treffen. Sowohl in der komplexen Ikonografie der Bilder als auch im Einsatz spezieller kinematografischer Mittel wird dies sichtbar.

Anoir and the Woman in the Garden (2015–2017) zählt mit seiner großen epischen Kraft zu den Hauptwerken in Patricia Reinharts Filmœuvre und zeigt die Schönheit ethisch-politischer Werte (verkörpert von einer Frau in einem weißen Kleid), das Machtego (dargestellt durch einen Pfau), apokalyptischen Untergang (visualisiert durch ein explosionsartiges Inferno des Terrors) und Lösungsversuche nach dem Ende der Welt in Gestalt einer dem Meer entsteigenden nackten Frau. Sie repräsentiert das gezeichnete Bild einer Zukunftsversion. Querverweise zur griechischen Mythologie – Europa, Tochter des Königs Agenor, die von dem in einen Stier verwandelten Zeus entführt wird – skizzieren den Übergang von einer patriarchischen zu einer matriarchalischen Ordnung. Bilder von Statuen, die Frauen als Kriegerinnen zeigen, eine auf die Malerin Frida Kahlo referenzierende Frauenfigur in einem labyrinthischen Garten aus phallusartigen, brennenden Kakteen (Bild der sich auflehnenden Künstlerin in einem patriarchalen System) oder vor einer Bucht mit einem Spiegel in der Hand neben Fruchtbarkeit symbolisierenden Lilien, Szenen einer Mutter mit Baby inmitten eines paradiesischen Gartens (dessen Dreh- und Locationmaterial aus Monets Garten in Giverny entspringt), in dem sich eine in einem Spiegel reflektierende Hölle kristallisiert, werden in dichte Bild- und Soundsequenzen gespannt. Patricia Reinharts außerordentliche Fähigkeit, dramaturgisch referenzreiche Inhalte geradezu opernhaft mit visueller Opulenz zu inszenieren, ist getragen von der Leidenschaft, mit komplexen Arrangements der Bildkomposition selbst an riskanten Schauplätzen (gedreht wurde an den Klippen der Küste rund um Marseille und auf Mallorca) zu arbeiten. Patricia Reinhart nützt den Landschaftsraum als Bühne, bezieht die Unberechenbarkeit der Natur als Kulisse in ihre Choreografie ein. „Max Ernsts Collagen aus *Une semaine de bonté* [von 1934] zeigten mir Möglichkeiten, neue Bühnen einer apokalyptischen Welt zu gestalten."[5] Das Wasser des Meeres wird zum Sinnbild eines Überlebenskampfes zwischen Tod, Erlösung und Wiedergeburt. *Anoir and the Woman in the Garden* ist ein künstlerischer Kurzfilm, der in seiner ikonografischen Dichte Anknüpfungspunkte zur Reflexionstheorie der Moral sichtbar werden lässt. Als moralische Instanz und letzte Überlebende nach dem Ende der Welt repräsentiert eine in der Felsenlandschaft auftauchende Nonne das Gute und den Glauben an die Welt. Als rätselhaftes weibliches Pendant zu *Der Mönch am Meer* (1808–1810) von Caspar David Friedrich blickt sie, eine radikale Einsamkeit ausstrahlend, auf das Meer. Doch selbst sie hat angesichts des vom Menschen verursachten Infernos den Glauben verloren. Was folgt, ist der Freitod. Wie ist dieser scheinbare Gegensatz zwischen der Ankunft in einer „postmoralischen" Zeit und der gleichzeitigen Anerkennung der Unerlässlichkeit einer angewandten Ethik zu verstehen? In der Kompromisslosigkeit, mit der gegen das politische und religiöse Establishment angekämpft wird, existieren Parallelen zu Pier Paolo Pasolinis Film *Il Vangelo secondo Matteo* (1964). *Anoir and the Woman in the Garden* ist als visuelles Musikstück komponiert und rhythmisch mit dem elektronischen Sound von Frédéric D. Oberland geschnitten, dessen Originalversion Patricia Reinhart durch in die Länge gezogene Verzerrungen veränderte. Durch den so bewirkten zeitlichen Transfer und akustischen Spiegel schafft sie eine weitere unsere Sinne fesselnde Dimension. Der Organismus des Films gewinnt durch das Zusammenspiel von Performance-, Film- und Soundtechniken an magischer Intensität.

Patricia Reinharts eigener Körper als performativer Handlungsträger bezieht sich nicht nur auf das, was biologisch gesprochen menschlich und lebendig und deshalb auch sterblich ist, sondern auf sowohl historische wie auch gegenwärtige Manifestationen einer immer noch zunehmenden Komplexität von Handlungsmacht. Um neue Narrative vorstellbar und Raum möglich zu machen für eine verbundene, komplizierte und komplexe Realität, bedient sich Patricia Reinhart der Metapher des Todes. Sie muss immer einen Schritt voraus sein.

Wie Filmanalyse und filmische Produktion ineinanderfließen, zeigt das Werk *13 Poèmes visibles (Ophélia & Avant de mourir)* (2011). Im Original laufen die 13 Super-8-Filme in Loops, die zwischen 8 und 35 Sekunden lang sind, als Rauminstallation parallel und bilden ein fast orchestrales Arrangement. Das diesem sinfonischen Aufeinandertreffen von 13 Frauenporträts zugrunde liegende Konzept ist inspiriert von der Publikation *Speaking about Godard*[6], die auf Gesprächen zwischen der feministischen Filmtheoretikerin Kaja Silverman – vom Poststrukturalismus und der Psychoanalyse kommend – und dem Avantgarde-Filmemacher Harun Farocki über Godards wichtigste Filme und deren formale und theoretische Innovationen basiert. Im Kapitel *Nana ist ein Tier* wird Godards Film *Vivre sa vie* von ihnen quergelesen, indem sie jede Szene detailliert durchbesprechen. Patricia Reinhart knüpft an diese Filmanalysen an: „Dieses Gespräch führte mich zu den Bildern und fungierte als eine Art Werkzeug, sodass ich darin für mich eine neue Ordnung sah, die mir eine Struktur gab, um meinen Ideen ein konzeptuelles ‚Korsett der Form' zu geben, das ich für die *Poèmes* brauchte."[7] Im analogen Experimentieren mit Super-8-Filmmaterial und im bewussten Einsatz der Empfindlichkeit des Materials Film werden Gebrauchsspuren – Riss, Durchbrennen, Abnützung – als ästhetische Form eingesetzt, um die Dramatik der eigentlichen menschlichen Fragilität darzustellen.

Es sind historische, literarische und filmische Referenzen, mit denen Patricia Reinhart den Weg in die Gegenwart spannt. Ihre Szene der Jeanne d'Arc bezieht sich auf den Historienfilm *La Passion de Jeanne d'Arc* von Carl Theodor Dreyer aus dem Jahr 1928. 1962 realisierte Jean-Luc Godard seinen vierten Spielfilm *Vivre sa vie: film en douze tableaux*, einen essayistischen, dokumentarischen Bericht über den Alltag der jungen Prostituierten Nana, in dem Godards damalige Ehefrau, Anna Karina, die Hauptrolle spielte. Etwa 14 Minuten nach Beginn des Films sehen wir Nana in einem Kino sitzen, wo sie eine besonders pointierte, transzendentale Szene aus Carl Theodor Dreyers Meisterwerk mit Maria Falconetti in der Hauptrolle anschaut. Sie zeigt Jeanne d'Arc, die auf ihren Tod wartet. Patricia Reinhart bezieht sich auf diese Szenen aus Godards Film und Dreyers Meisterwerk. Sie ist an der Dramatik dieser Frauenfigur interessiert, die, obwohl sie alles richtig machte in der Männerwelt, in der sie agierte, und Frankreich zum Sieg verholfen hatte, der Ketzerei bezichtigt, verurteilt und hingerichtet wurde. Dieses Bild von Frau, die zu Unrecht starb und dies gleichzeitig aufgrund ihrer religiösen Erziehung selbst akzeptierte, bildet eine der insgesamt 13 Sequenzen, die in Patricia Reinharts Inszenierung von Stummfilmstars wie Asta Nielsen, Lyda Borelli oder Pola Negri inspiriert sind. Extravagante Frauen im Rampenlicht, die als Diven galten und als „Göttliche" verehrt wurden und deren selbstbewusste Ambitionen zur Selbstermächtigung oft dramatisch mit dem frühen Tod endeten. Die dazu verfassten Subtexte handeln von Tod und Erlösung, von der Konfrontation mit den anderen, referieren auf Virginia Woolfs *A Room of One's Own* (1929)[8], hinterfragen, wie sich Perspektiven für Freiheit, Eigenverantwortung und Visionen öffnen, thematisieren Gewalt, die Frage nach Opfer- und Täter:innenrollen. Es begegnen uns selbstbestimmte Frauen, die an äußeren Umständen scheitern. Eine kurze, 13 Sekunden lange Sequenz zeigt, wie die Frau erschossen wird und das Blut aus ihrem Oberkörper fließt. „Werden nicht sämtliche Träume und Visionen in diesem System sofort zunichtegemacht?",[9] fragt Patricia Reinhart. Aus welchen Verstrickungen gilt es sich zu befreien? Warum werden historische Opern- und Theaterstücke nach wie vor in Versionen aufgeführt, in denen die Heldinnen meist dem Tod geweiht sind? Die von Patricia Reinhart filmisch inszenierte Figur der Ophelia bezieht sich auf ein Gemälde von John Everett Millais (1852) und auf die gleichnamige Figur in *Hamlet* (um 1600–1602), das zu den bis dato umstrittensten Werken von William Shakespeare zählt. Es existieren unterschiedliche Adaptionen, in denen die Liebesbeziehung zwischen Ophelia und Hamlet angezweifelt wird. Asta Nielsen übernahm 1921 die Titelrolle und spielte als erste Schauspielerin eine Frau, die sich als Mann verkleidete, womit sie Hamlet einer Geschlechtsumwandlung unterzog. „Dieser Film mit Asta Nielsen hat mich zu den Figuren geführt – ihre eigene seltsame schauspielerische Interpretation und Umsetzung, im Besonderen ihre steifen Armbewegungen von oben nach unten in einer Szene",[10] erläutert Patricia Reinhart ihr intensives Studium der Stummfilmstars, deren Karriere durch den Wechsel zum Tonfilm abrupt endete.

Patricia Reinhart nimmt zwei Aspekte gleichzeitig in den Blick: einerseits ihre Authentizität als Künstlerin, andererseits die gesellschaftlichen Bedingungen für Frauen, beides spannt sie in eine kulturhistorische Genealogie. Der Widerspruch zwischen der Prekarität ihrer Protagonistinnen und der Lust an einer Bildopulenz ist frappierend. Diesem widersprüchlichen Vexierbild könnte mit dem von Michel Foucault geprägten Konzept der Heterotopie begegnet werden, mit dessen Hilfe Patricia Reinhart eine Beziehung zwischen den utopischen, imaginierten Dimensionen ihrer real miteinander in keinem Zusammenhang stehenden Bilder und ihren materiellen, greifbaren Dimensionen herstellt. Heterotopie könnte im Zusammenhang von Patricia Reinharts *Ciné Collagen*, angewendet auf die Dreikanalvideoinstallation *Ein Nachtstück* (2011/12),

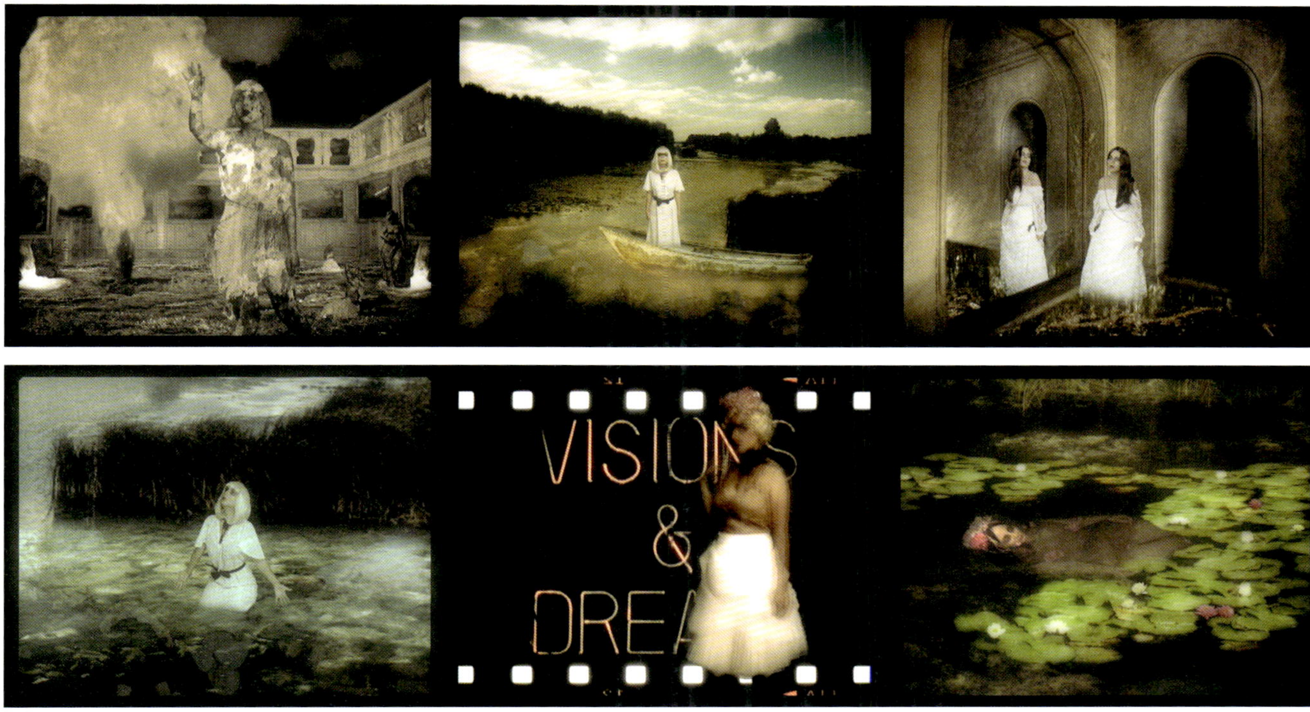

13 Poèmes visibles (Ophélia & Avant de mourir), Super-8 film installation and Ciné Collage, 2011

als Visualisierung imaginärer Orte und Parallelwelten gesehen werden, die Raum für neue Erfahrungshorizonte öffnen. Die *Ciné Collage* als Heterotopie schafft eine Illusion der scheinbaren (Alb-)Traumhaftigkeit. „In *Ein Nachtstück* taucht eine weibliche Figur in Peter Doigs Kanu auf",[11] gibt Patricia Reinhart Einblick in die in ihren Filmen existierenden Referenzen, die wie subtile Zitate in ihre Filmsequenzen mit eingewoben werden. Diese Stränge sind wie Fäden, die sich verknüpfen. Aufgenommen in Paris, zeigt Patricia Reinhart in ihrer Visualisierung, wie Vergangenheit in Form einer „historischen Gegenwart" in Gebäuden überlebt und so Vergangenheit und Gegenwart gleichzeitig stattfinden.

Der Wahrnehmungsakt gestaltet sich zu einer Enthüllung, zu einem Moment der Differenz. Ich weiß, dass das, was ich sehe, zwar nicht real ist, doch mich der Wirklichkeit näherbringt. Patricia Reinharts künstlerische Unabhängigkeit besteht darin, auch gegenüber den angewandten Techniken kritisch zu sein und ihnen Fantasien der Machbarkeit gegenüberzustellen. Im Prozess der filmischen Ausarbeitung ist sie eine visuelle Exzentrikerin, sie arbeitet ohne Drehbuch, mit Skizzen an der visuellen Maximierung ihrer Filme, in denen sich Standbilder und Videosequenzen wie Elementarteilchen aneinanderfügen und kategorische Abgrenzungen sich auflösen. Ihrem explosiven visuellen Gestaltungswillen entwachsen essayistische Abhandlungen eines unberechenbaren Werks und eine skeptische Haltung gegenüber dem modernen Glauben, durch Bildkonstruktionen der Realität habhaft zu werden.

In ihren frühen Kurzfilmen inszeniert Patricia Reinhart humorvolle Porträts, Alltagsszenen und Slapsticks, die vom Charme der Stummfilmzeit durchdrungen sind. Sie beherrscht die Kunst der Verwandlung, mit ihrem schauspielerischen Talent und einem natürlichen Gefühl für Komik, schönen Grimassen in der Manier der Anfänge des Films in selbst gebauten Miniatursets mit Requisiten. Sie nutzt die medialen Praktiken, die Fotografie und Film gemeinsam haben, nämlich die Fokussierung von einem bestimmten Standpunkt aus, zur Inszenierung und Manipulation durch die Rahmensetzung und die Optionen der Selbstreflexion des eigenen medialen Verfahrens. Auf ihre Recherchen zur Filmemacherin Maya Deren, zu deren experimentellen Filmen aus den 1940er-Jahren und der Entwicklung der spezifischen Kunstform des Videotanzes folgt eine intensive Auseinandersetzung mit Maya Derens Filmtheorien und einem filmischen Denken, das intersensorische Welten eröffnet. Wie in Maya Derens Filmen ist im filmischen Œuvre von Patricia Reinhart ein großer Teil der kreativen Handlung durch die Manipulation von Zeit und Raum sowohl in der Vorproduktion als auch in der Postproduktion präsent.

Patricia Reinhart bedient die Kamera mittels Stativ und Selbstauslöser, der intime Moment (des vollkommenen Alleinseins), die Suche nach dem authentischen Bild des Seins sind während des Drehs, der Inszenierung im öffentlichen Raum, essenziell. Im Studio arrangiert sie Fotosequenzen in der Manier der *Ciné Collage*, die es ihr ermöglicht, selbst mehrfach kaleidoskopartig ins Bild zu treten, sich einem hegemonialen Sehdispositiv zu widersetzen

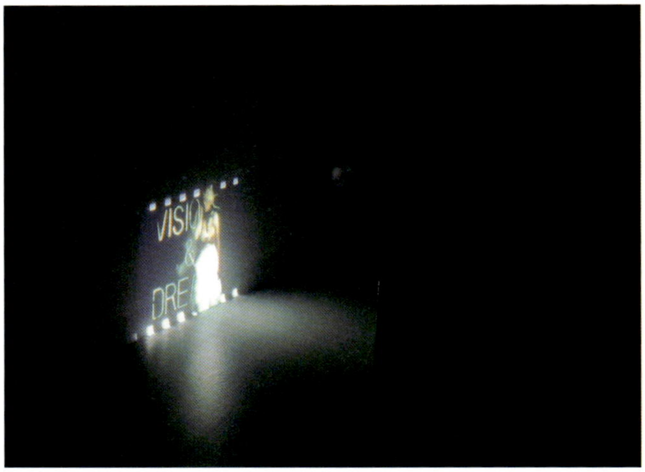

Exhibition view / Ausstellungsansicht / Vue de l'exposition
Avant de mourir, Galerie Lisa Ruyter, Vienna, 2011
13 Poèmes visibles (Ophélia & Avant de mourir), 2011

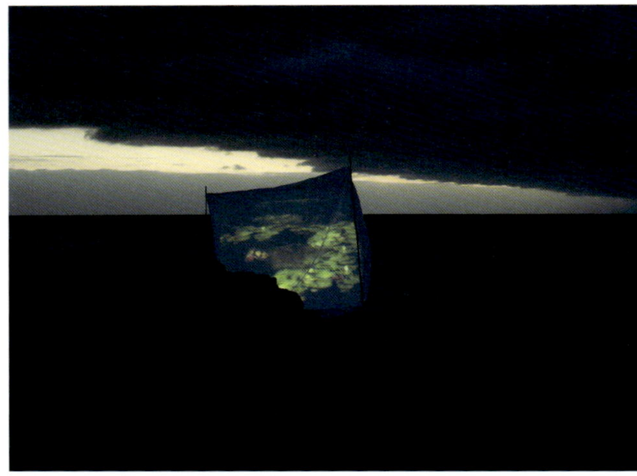

Screening at the beach / Filmvorführung am Strand / Projection à la plage, Cala LLamp, Mallorca, 2012
13 Poèmes visibles (Ophélia & Avant de mourir), 2011

und einen feministischen Impetus darin zu zeigen, Blickordnungen, Dominanzverhältnisse, Wahrnehmungs- und Visualisierungskonventionen aufzubrechen. Anknüpfend an die Filmtheoretikerin Kaja Silverman, lässt sich mit dem Begriff des Blickregimes auch die (Rück-)Wirkung von Wahrnehmungsstrukturen auf die Konstitution von Subjekt und damit von Geschlecht erfassen; insofern kann diese insistierende Auseinandersetzung mit konventionellen Blickstrukturen als kulturelle Praxis gesehen werden. Aus der dadurch entwickelten eigenen postdramatischen Ästhetik entstehen poetische Bildsequenzen, die durch die Montage zum Film werden – an der Schnittstelle zwischen Performance, Kunst und Filmgeschichte.

Was daraus folgt? Vielleicht, dass wir uns fragen müssen, wie sehr unsere derzeitige Kunst- und Literaturpraxis für neue Realismen, die ein Verhältnis zur Wirklichkeit unterhalten, Nährstoff gibt. Dass wir uns fragen, wie der Abstand zwischen dem Möglichen und dem Wirklichen überbrückt werden kann. Patricia Reinhart agiert in ihren Filmen wie ein Romancier, indem sie ihre Charaktere formt, die couragiert einer Passion folgen, deren selbstreferenzielles Potenzial sich zuspitzt und gleichzeitig Blickregime subversiv untergräbt.

Ursula Maria Probst ist Kunsthistorikerin, Kunstkritikerin, Künstlerin und freie Kuratorin für Fluc, KÖR, Public Art Niederösterreich, freiraum MQ. 2019–2022 Kuratorin für das AIR-Programm *Body Embedding* Österreich/Südostasien. 2013–2019 Billboardprojekt *Transcultural Emancipation*, KulturKontakt Austria / BKA / Fluc. 2016–2019 FLUCA österreichischer Kulturpavillon, Plovdiv, Bulgarien. 2016 Curator-in-Residence in Rio de Janeiro. 2015 Kuratorin der österreichischen Beiträge der Havanna Biennale. Vorträge und Projekte u. a. in Myanmar, Slowenien, Vietnam, Ukraine, Russland, China, Zypern.

1 Arno Gruen, *Der Verrat am Selbst. Die Angst vor Autonomie bei Mann und Frau*, München 1986.
2 Shoshana Felman, *The Literary Speech Act. Don Juan with J. L. Austin, or Seduction in Two Languages*, Ithaca, NY, 1983.
3 Judith Butler, *Gender Trouble. Feminism and the Subversion of Identity*, New York 1990.
4 Patricia Reinhart im Gespräch im November 2021.
5 Ebd.
6 Kaja Silverman, Harun Farocki, *Speaking about Godard*, New York 1998.
7 Patricia Reinhart im Gespräch im November 2021.
8 Virginia Woolf, *Ein Zimmer für sich allein* (1929), Berlin 1978.
9 Patricia Reinhart im Gespräch im November 2021.
10 Ebd.
11 Ebd.

Réajuster le regard
Réflexion sur la réfraction : la femme multidimensionnelle
The (Re)birth of HER_story

Ursula Maria Probst

Les frontières entre réalité et fiction sont poreuses dans un environnement où l'information circule en accéléré – l'imagination joue un rôle croissant. Que se passerait-il si, au lieu de raconter l'histoire de la chute de notre société depuis un état idyllique, nous nous demandions comment nous en sommes arrivés à être enfermés dans des carcans conceptuels si étroits que nous n'imaginons même plus pouvoir nous réinventer ?

L'œuvre de Patricia Reinhart incorpore des citations du psychanalyste et critique social Arno Gruen. Dans sa théorie sur la lutte humaine pour la survie, il met en garde contre une culture du non-être et contre la perte de l'empathie entre humains. Selon Gruen, penser sans empathie conduit à un monde illusoire fait d'abstractions, à travers lesquelles la réalité n'est plus appréhendée de façon immédiate et avec la compassion nécessaire.[1]

Dans ses films, Patricia Reinhart place sous une focale critique les processus de subjectivation et les pratiques de construction et de superposition des inégalités réelles ainsi que de l'ordre binaire des sexes. Par une recherche artistique qui interroge de manière transdisciplinaire des sources issues de la littérature, de l'histoire de l'art, de la théorie du cinéma, de la psychologie et de la sociologie, elle plonge dans la complexité du comportement humain et des constructions spécifiques au genre. Le moteur de son œuvre filmée est l'identité féminine comme processus permanent de négociation entre les images de soi et des autres, entre les normes de genre, les modèles et les représentations culturelles associées à la féminité.

Patricia Reinhart confronte sa vision à celle des économies actuelles de l'image et du regard pour développer sa pratique qu'elle nomme « Ciné Collage ». Un processus de création inspiré par *La Jetée* (1962), film de science-fiction politique dont Chris Marker a réalisé la conception et le montage à partir de photographies fixes. Elle produit des films dont l'esthétique de fin du monde rappelle celle d'Andreï Tarkovski, et adapte les méthodes visuelles du test projectif de Rorschach (test de la tâche d'encre) utilisé en psychodiagnostic. Ces séquences cinématographiques fonctionnent comme des reflets, donnent forme à la notion d'images comme miroir et amènent à réfléchir de manière critique aux thèses de Jacques Lacan sur le devenir du sujet – le stade du miroir comme formateur de la fonction du Je. La critique féministe de Shoshana Felman[2] et Judith Butler[3] l'a discuté avec vigueur : le modèle lacanien des processus de subjectivation ne vaut pas de la même manière pour les deux sexes, car il reste subordonné chez Lacan au « primat du phallus », qui renvoie toujours la femme au lieu de l'Autre. Judith Butler a ensuite analysé l'hétéronormativité de la psychanalyse structurale d'inspiration lacanienne, et oppose son concept de performativité à la conception psychanalytique de l'acceptation du genre. La méthode de Patricia Reinhart consiste à combiner des images fixes sélectionnées dans ses archives pour créer sur la surface du film un affrontement constant entre les motifs abstraits et les corps ou les paysages figuratifs, de la faune et de la flore. Au-delà d'une détermination hétéronormative du film, cela active le domaine spéculatif du potentiel d'émancipation pour nous rapprocher de nouvelles narrations.

La création cinématographique de Patricia Reinhart est une « One-Woman Production ». Elle est autrice, actrice, photographe, cadreuse, réalisatrice. En outre, en raison de l'utilisation de techniques cinématographiques complexes – fondées sur l'étude des techniques du film muet, du dessin animé et de la Nouvelle Vague – nous pourrions ajouter que c'est une « One-Woman Post-Production ». Elle est impliquée personnellement à chaque étape : en studio cinéma, lors de prises de vues en bord de piscine, de mer, de paysages ou dans l'espace public. Elle y affirme un critère important de son intégrité artistique. Ses débuts se caractérisent par une spontanéité joueuse et par un désir impossible à réprimer pour l'étude des caractères et l'articulation des gestes et expressions faciales associés à des rôles et figures de femmes dans l'histoire, la littérature ou la société. Ainsi, la pose, comme zone intermédiaire entre suggestion et désignation, comme figure exemplaire de la transition, comme imbrication de la mise en scène entre soi et l'imagerie, donne un poids à son œuvre actuelle d'une conceptualité épique. Elle combine les effets spéciaux du *Ciné Collage* qu'elle a développés – d'abord pour le stop-motion, puis reconfigurés pour le présent – avec des actions mises en scène dont elle est la protagoniste. Ces processus combinés s'entrecroisent avec différents détails de lieux, de scènes historiques, d'éléments architecturaux et sculpturaux. Cette fusion hybride donne lieu à des séquences animées faisant apparaitre un monde virtuel hypnotique et inédit.

Dès la genèse de son travail, Patricia Reinhart donne à voir comment différents systèmes, actions, émotions peuvent se superposer et comment les gestes et les émotions sont intégrés dans les relations. Elle développe des techniques qui permettent à ses personnages – principalement incarnés par elle, tandis qu'elle est démultipliée dans l'image – d'interagir. A la recherche d'interfaces entre la vie individuelle et la mémoire de l'humanité, dans un dialogue sur la condition et représentation féminine, Patricia Reinhart poursuit un usage vigilant, poétique et politique du médium cinématographique et de ses innovations techniques.

Ciné Collage est le nom pertinent pour ce procédé de superposition, qui transfère la technique du collage sur le film tandis que le montage des images provoque une réflexion métafictionnelle du récit. De nouvelles formes visuelles apparaissent et affrontent les conventions cinématographiques. Patricia Reinhart se nourrit des différentes sources pour opérer des glissements de sens poétiques à travers le *Ciné Collage*. La perception qu'elle a d'elle-même comme peintre travaillant par strates se transpose dans le médium cinématographique, ce qui augmente la profondeur des couleurs et des formes. Elle tire son vocabulaire cinématographique de sa pratique picturale, mais aussi de ses compétences de comédienne. Parallèlement à ses études de peinture, elle a étudié le jeu théâtral. Afin d'éviter tout conflit concernant les droits d'auteur, elle a décidé dès ses débuts d'utiliser son propre matériel, ses images fixes et ses tournages vidéo. Elle dispose désormais de vastes archives comprenant jusqu'à 500 photos par thème. Elle photographie à plusieurs reprises des images uniques pour briser l'illusion de continuité du film résultant du montage d'images fixes. Les moments figés qu'elle crée ainsi font écho au silence de la pellicule et soulignent l'incroyable vitalité de ses films.

Avec son regard acéré, Patricia Reinhart analyse filmiquement les inégalités de traitement qui se manifestent dans la vie réelle et se reflètent dans la littérature, le cinéma et l'art. Elle fait appel à des processus d'émancipation et réalise des performances en se glissant dans d'innombrables rôles de femmes, de personnages historiques et littéraires – comme l'Ophélie de Shakespeare ou la Jeanne d'Arc de Dreyer – qui lui servent à questionner l'identité féminine dans des contextes sociaux spécifiques ou à restituer métaphoriquement des phénomènes sociaux. Après avoir étudié le cinéma muet, ses techniques de création d'illusions visuelles, ainsi que le cinéma d'animation, elle s'est intéressée de près à la Nouvelle Vague, notamment à Jean-Luc Godard et ses personnages féminins interprétés par Anna Karina – en particulier dans *Vivre sa vie* (1962), *Alphaville* (1965) et *Pierrot le fou* (1965). « Cette esthétique cinématographique des années 1960 m'a amenée à mes autoportraits, réalisés exclusivement dans les photomatons parisiens », explique Patricia Reinhart en faisant le lien avec son œuvre photographique. « En outre, les *Untitled Film Stills* de Cindy Sherman [des années 1977 à 1980] m'ont par la suite inspiré pour mes séquences de films. »[4]

Les images ne (re)produisent pas seulement le visible, mais suggèrent aussi les normes dominantes. Avec son analyse des régimes de regard qui déterminent ce qui apparaît à l'écran dans le répertoire culturel des images, la théoricienne féministe du cinéma Kaja Silverman fournit un indice sur les paramètres de représentation. Comment réagir au fait d'être reflétée et comment réussir à résister à une appropriation du soi par les images ? Dans cette perspective critique de la représentation, Patricia Reinhart développe ses propres procédés, nous permettant d'accéder à d'autres images. Celles qui, grâce aux techniques développées, prennent une distance productive par rapport à ce qui est déjà donné à voir. A l'instar de Chantal Akerman, réinventrice de formes cinématographiques, Patricia Reinhart, suivant son propre féminisme, développe une nouvelle dramaturgie qui transgresse les frontières entre les genres avec un sens aigu de la durée et de l'expérience temporelle.

Les trois œuvres décrites ci-dessous sont issues d'un cycle filmique apocalyptique. Patricia Reinhart développe cette thématique depuis plus de dix ans pour explorer l'expression d'une possible fin du monde. On compte dans cette série des films comme *Die ihr Brot mit Tränen aß (Requiem for an Unendurable Paradise)* (2013/2014) et *Kirkirerland* (2008). La question centrale est : comment vivre en portant

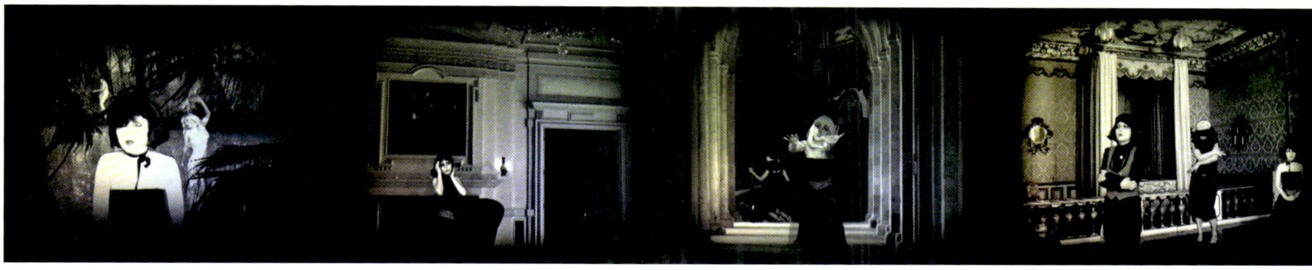

Nocturne in Black, Ciné Collage, 2008

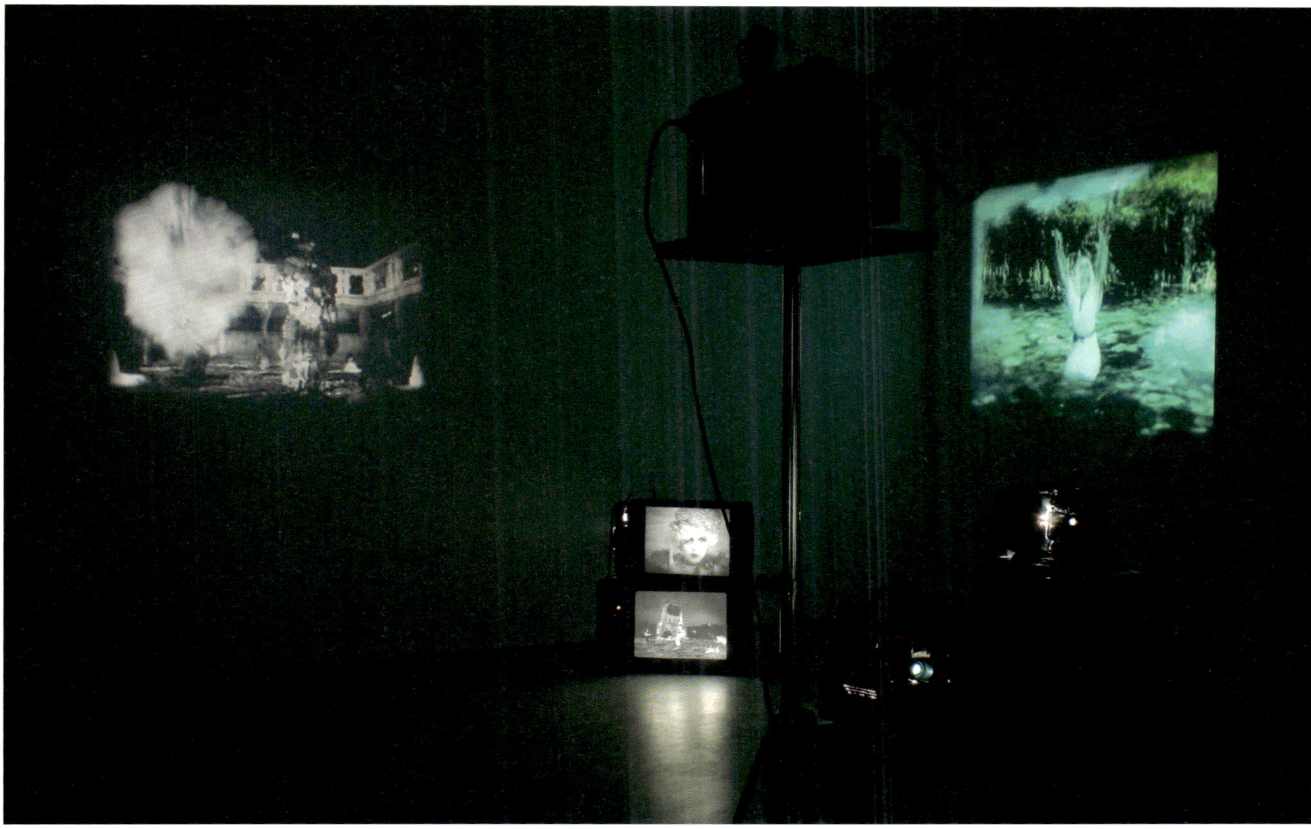

Exhibition view / Ausstellungsansicht / Vue de l'exposition *Avant de mourir*, Galerie Lisa Ruyter, Vienna, 2011
13 Poèmes visibles (Ophélia & Avant de mourir), Super-8 film installation, 2011

en soi une mort inéluctable ; comment se comporter face à la fin du monde ? Il s'agit en partie d'acceptation, en partie d'une lutte pour la survie ou d'un désespoir à la recherche d'un avenir différent que nous rencontrons dans ses films. C'est visible tant dans l'iconographie complexe des images que dans l'utilisation de moyens cinématographiques spécifiques.

Anoir and the Woman in the Garden (2015–2017) compte parmi les pièces principales de l'œuvre cinématographique de Patricia Reinhart. Ce film d'une grande force épique explore la beauté des valeurs politiques, éthiques (incarnées par une femme en robe blanche), de l'égo du pouvoir (représenté par un paon), de la catastrophe apocalyptique (visualisée dans un enfer explosif de terreur) et des tentatives de solutions post fin du monde incarnés par une femme nue surgissant de la mer, allégorie d'un possible avenir. Des références empruntées à la mythologie grecque – dans laquelle Europe, fille du roi Agénor, a été enlevée par Zeus transformé en taureau – esquissent le passage d'un ordre patriarcal à un ordre matriarcal. Telles ces statues, les femmes se dressent tout au long de denses séquences visuelles et acoustiques. Elles incarnent des guerrières, une figure féminine renvoyant à la peintre Frida Kahlo dans un jardin labyrinthique de cactus brûlants aux formes phalliques (image de l'artiste féminine se rebellant dans un système patriarcal) ou, un miroir à la main, devant une baie, à côté d'un lys symbolisant la fertilité, puis une mère et son bébé au milieu d'un jardin paradisiaque (celui de Monet à Giverny). Des scènes féminines où se cristallise un enfer se réfléchissant dans un miroir. L'habileté fascinante de Patricia Reinhart à mettre en scène des contenus

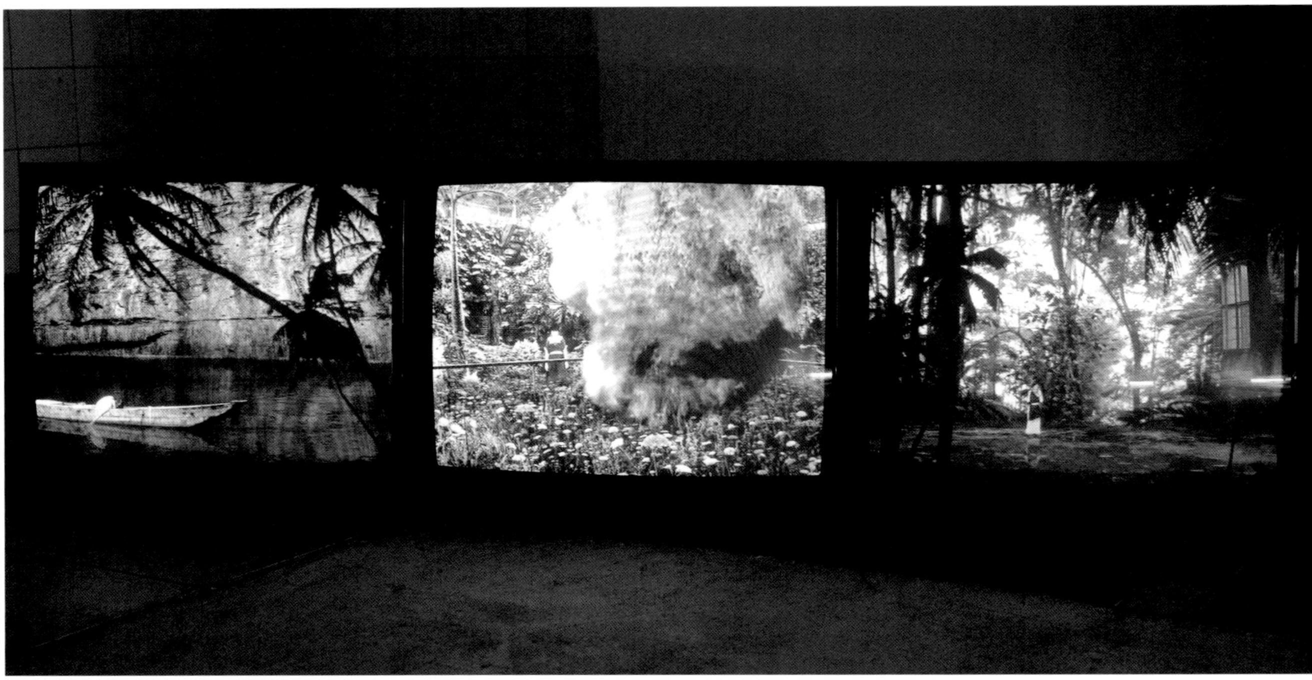

Exhibition view / Ausstellungsansicht / Vue de l'exposition *Predicting Memories*, Vienna Art Week, Vienna, 2012
Ein Nachtstück, three-channel video installation, Ciné Collage, 2011/12

dramaturgiques riches de références visuelles opératiques est portée par une passion pour un travail de composition et d'arrangement d'images filmées dans des conditions risquées (dans les falaises près de Marseille et à Majorque). Patricia Reinhart utilise les paysages comme scène, et fait de l'imprévisibilité de la nature les coulisses de sa chorégraphie. « Les collages de Max Ernst dans *Une semaine de bonté* [de 1943] m'ont montré les possibilités de former de nouvelles scènes d'un monde apocalyptique. »[5] L'eau de la mer devient le symbole d'un combat pour la survie entre mort, rédemption et renaissance. Dans *Anoir and the Woman in the Garden*, court-métrage artistique, la densité iconographique laisse apparaître les contours d'une théorie réflexive de la morale. Une nonne, surgissant dans un paysage rocheux, incarne l'instance morale, la dernière survivante après la fin du monde. Elle représente d'abord le bien et la foi dans le monde. Énigmatique pendant féminin inspiré par *Der Mönch am Meer* (1808–1810) de Caspar David Friedrich, elle regarde la mer debout dans sa solitude radicale. Pourtant, même elle a perdu la foi face à l'enfer déclenché par l'homme. Ce qui suit est son suicide. Comment comprendre ce paradoxe apparent entre l'arrivée dans un monde « post-moral » et la reconnaissance simultanée du caractère indispensable d'une éthique appliquée ? On peut tracer un parallèle avec le film de Pier Paolo Pasolini, *Il Vangelo secondo Matteo* (1964) dans l'absence de compromis avec laquelle est combattu l'establishment politique et religieux. *Anoir and the Woman in the Garden* est composé comme une pièce musicale visuelle, rythmé par le son électronique de Frédéric D. Oberland. Patricia Reinhart déforme ce matériel sonore en ajoutant des distorsions étirées, qui créent une nouvelle dimension en modifiant nos perceptions temporelles et en décuplant ainsi le miroir acoustique. Grâce à l'interaction entre différentes techniques performatives, image et son prennent vie comme un organisme vivant d'une grande intensité mystique.

Le propre corps de Patricia Reinhart, en tant que support performatif de l'action, ne se réfère pas seulement à ce qui est, biologiquement parlant, humain et vivant – et donc aussi mortel – mais aussi aux manifestations d'une complexité toujours croissante du pouvoir d'action actuel et passé. Afin d'imaginer un néo-récit et d'ouvrir l'espace vers une réalité connectée et complexe, elle a recours à la métaphore de la mort. Elle semble animée par la volonté d'avoir toujours un temps d'avance sur le présent.

L'œuvre *13 Poèmes visibles (Ophélia & Avant de mourir)* (2011) montre comment l'analyse de film et la production cinématographique s'entremêlent. L'œuvre originale est une installation spatiale dans laquelle treize films Super-8 sont lancés en parallèle dans des boucles de huit à trente cinq secondes, formant un arrangement quasi-orchestral. Le concept sous-jacent à la rencontre symphonique de treize portraits de femmes s'inspire de *Speaking about Godard*[6]. Cette suite d'entretiens entre la théoricienne féministe du cinéma Kaja Silverman – issue du poststructuralisme et de la psychanalyse – et le cinéaste d'avant-garde Harun

Farocki traite des principaux films de Godard et de leurs innovations formelles et théoriques. Dans le chapitre *Nana est une bête*, ils font une lecture croisée du film *Vivre sa vie* de Godard, en passant en revue chaque scène en détail. Patricia Reinhart se réfère à leurs analyses : « Cette conversation m'a menée aux images et a fonctionné comme une sorte d'outil, de sorte que j'y ai vu pour moi un nouvel ordre, qui m'a donné une structure pour donner à mes idées un ‹ corset de forme › conceptuel dont j'avais besoin pour les *Poèmes.* »[7] Dans l'expérimentation analogique sur de la pellicule Super-8 et dans l'utilisation consciente de la fragilité du matériau filmique (déchirure, brûlure, usure), les traces d'utilisation sont maniées comme forme esthétique pour représenter le drame de la fragilité humaine.

Patricia Reinhart utilise des références historiques, littéraires et cinématographiques pour tracer un chemin clair vers le présent. Sa scène de Jeanne d'Arc se réfère à *La Passion de Jeanne d'Arc*, film historique réalisé par Carl Theodor Dreyer en 1928. En 1962, Jean-Luc Godard réalisa son quatrième long métrage, *Vivre sa vie : film en douze tableaux*, récit essayiste et documentaire sur le quotidien de la jeune prostituée Nana, dans lequel son épouse de l'époque, Anna Karina, tenait le rôle principal. Environ quatorze minutes après le début du film, nous voyons Nana assise dans un cinéma où elle assiste à une scène particulièrement pointue et épique du chef-d'œuvre de Carl Theodor Dreyer, avec Maria Falconetti dans le rôle principal. Elle montre Jeanne d'Arc attendant la mort. Patricia Reinhart se réfère à la mise en scène de Godard et Dreyer. Elle s'intéresse au drame de cette figure féminine qui, bien qu'agissant héroïquement dans un monde d'hommes pour protéger et mener la France à la victoire, a été accusée d'hérésie, condamnée et exécutée. Cette image d'une femme morte injustement, acceptant son destin en raison de son éducation religieuse, constitue l'une des treize séquences dont la mise en scène s'inspire de stars du cinéma muet comme Asta Nielsen, Lyda Borelli ou Pola Negri. Des femmes extravagantes sous les feux de la rampe, considérées comme des divas et vénérées comme des « divinités », dont les ambitions affirmées d'indépendance et d'émancipation les ont souvent guidées, de manière dramatique, vers une mort prématurée. Les sous-textes qui les accompagnent traitent de la mort et de la rédemption, de la confrontation avec les autres – faisant référence à *A Room of One's Own* (1929)[8] de Virginia Woolf. Ils nous interrogent sur la manière dont s'ouvrent des perspectives de liberté, de responsabilité personnelle et de vision, abordent le thème de la violence et influencent les rôles de victime et de coupable, masculins et/ou féminins. Nous y rencontrons des femmes autodéterminées qui échouent en raison de circonstances extérieures. Une courte séquence de treize secondes montre une femme abattue, le sang s'écoulant de son torse. « Tous les rêves et visions ne sont-ils pas irrémédiablement réduits à néant dans ce système ? »,[9] demande Patricia Reinhart. De quels enchevêtrements faut-il se libérer ? Pourquoi les opéras et les pièces de théâtre historiques continuent-ils à être les représentations de versions où les héroïnes sont le plus souvent vouées à la mort ? Le personnage d'Ophélie qu'elle met en scène dans son film évoque un tableau de John Everett Millais (1852) et fait référence à l'Ophélie de Shakespeare dans *Hamlet* (vers 1600–1602), qui compte parmi les œuvres les plus controversées de William Shakespeare à ce jour. Il existe différentes adaptations dans lesquelles la relation amoureuse entre Ophélie et Hamlet est mise en doute. Asta Nielsen a repris le rôle-titre en 1921 et a été la première comédienne à jouer une femme déguisée en homme, changeant le genre d'Hamlet. « Ce film avec Asta Nielsen m'a menée vers les personnages – son interprétation personnelle étrange de la transposition théâtrale, en particulier ses mouvements de bras raides de haut en bas dans une scène »,[10] explique Patricia Reinhart, forte de son observation intensive des stars du cinéma muet, dont la carrière s'est brutalement terminée lors du passage au cinéma parlant.

Patricia Reinhart nous révèle deux volontés fondamentales à son œuvre : d'une part sa grande intention d'authenticité artistique, d'autre part son besoin de mettre en lumière les conditions sociales des femmes, en les inscrivant dans une généalogie culturelle et historique. La contradiction entre la précarité de ses protagonistes et le désir d'une opulence d'images est frappante. Cette opposition pourrait être abordée à l'aide du concept d'hétérotopie forgé par Michel Foucault, selon lequel elle établit une relation entre les dimensions utopiques et imaginaires de ses images, qui n'ont aucun lien entre elles, et leurs dimensions matérielles tangibles. Dans ces *Ciné Collages*, en particulier dans l'installation vidéo à trois canaux *Ein Nachtstück* (2011/2012), on peut comprendre l'hétérotopie comme la visualisation de lieux imaginaires et de mondes parallèles qui ouvrent l'espace à de nouveaux horizons d'expérience. Le *Ciné Collage* en tant qu'hétérotopie crée une illusion, celle d'un (mauvais) rêve apparent. « Dans *Ein Nachtstück*, un personnage féminin apparaît dans le canoë de Peter Doig » :[11] Patricia Reinhart donne un aperçu des références qui existent dans ses films et qui se tissent comme des citations subtiles dans ses séquences cinématographiques. Ces brins sont comme des fils qui s'entrecroisent. Ses images capturées à Paris montrent un passé qui survit à la manière d'un « présent historique » dans ses architectures et monuments et qui incarne simultanément l'hier et l'aujourd'hui.

L'acte de perception devient révélation, moment de différence. Je sais que ce que je vois n'est pas réel, et pourtant cela me rapproche de la réalité. L'indépendance artistique de Patricia Reinhart consiste également à rester critique face aux techniques utilisées et à les opposer aux fantasmes de faisabilité. Dans le processus d'élaboration du film, elle impose sa vision insolite, travaille sans scénario et sur esquisses à la maximisation visuelle de ses films, dans lesquels images fixes et séquences vidéo s'assemblent comme des particules élémentaires où les délimitations catégoriques se dissolvent. Sa créativité visuelle détonante a donné lieu à l'élaboration d'une œuvre imprévisible et à une attitude sceptique à l'égard de la croyance moderne selon laquelle la réalité peut être appréhendée par des constructions d'images.

Dans ses premiers courts métrages, Patricia Reinhart met en scène des portraits humoristiques, des scènes de la vie quotidienne et des farces burlesques imprégnées du charme de l'époque du cinéma muet. Elle maîtrise l'art de la métamorphose. Avec une habileté d'actrice et un sens naturel de la comédie, ses singulières grimaces renvoient aux débuts du cinéma dans des décors miniatures qu'elle a elle-même construits avec des accessoires. Elle utilise les pratiques communes aux médias de la photographie et du cinéma : la focalisation à partir d'un point de vue précis pour mettre en scène et manipuler le cadre, et générer une réflexivité sur son propre usage du medium. Ses recherches sur la cinéaste Maya Deren, sur ses films expérimentaux des années 1940 et sur cette forme artistique induite spécifique à la vidéo-danse, ont débouché sur une étude intensive de ses théories et de sa pensée audiovisuelle qui ouvre des mondes intersensoriels. Comme dans les films de Maya Deren, l'œuvre cinématographique de Patricia Reinhart accueille une quantité généreuse d'action créative, qui gagne en force à travers la manipulation du temps et de l'espace, aussi bien dans la pré-production que dans la post-production.

Patricia Reinhart se sert de la caméra sur trépied avec retardateur : le moment intime (de la solitude parfaite), la recherche de l'image authentique de l'être sont essentiels pendant le tournage et la mise en scène dans l'espace public. En studio, elle arrange ses séquences photographiques à la manière du *Ciné Collage*, ce qui lui permet d'entrer elle-même plusieurs fois dans l'image comme dans l'œil d'un kaléidoscope, et de s'opposer à un dispositif visuel hégémonique. Elle affirme ainsi son élan féministe en brisant les ordres de regard, les rapports de domination, les conventions de perception et de visualisation. Suivant la théoricienne du cinéma Kaja Silverman, sa notion de régime de regard permet également de saisir l'effet (en retour) des structures de perception dans la constitution du sujet et donc du genre ; dans cette optique, cette confrontation avec les structures conventionnelles du regard peut être considérée comme une pratique culturelle. De l'esthétique post-dramatique ainsi développée naissent des séquences d'images poétiques qui, grâce au montage, deviennent des films – au croisement entre la performance, l'art et l'histoire du cinéma.

Quelle est la suite ? Peut-être devons-nous nous demander dans quelle mesure notre pratique artistique et littéraire actuelle nourrit de nouveaux réalismes qui entretiennent un rapport avec la réalité. Nous demander comment combler la distance entre le possible et le réel. Dans ses films, Patricia Reinhart agit comme une romancière, en façonnant ses personnages qui suivent courageusement une passion dont le potentiel autoréférentiel s'aiguise tout en subvertissant les régimes de regard.

Ursula Maria Probst est historienne de l'art, critique d'art, artiste et curatrice indépendante pour Fluc, KÖR, Public Art Niederösterreich, freiraum MQ. 2019–2022 curatrice pour le programme d'artistes en résidence *Body Embedding* Autriche/Asie du Sud-Est. 2013–2019 projet de billboard *Transcultural Emancipation*, KulturKontakt Austria / BKA / Fluc. 2016–2019 FLUCA, pavillon autrichien de la Culture, Plovdiv, Bulgarie. 2016 curatrice en résidence à Rio de Janeiro. 2015 curatrice des contributions autrichiennes à la Biennale de La Havane. Conférences et projets au Myanmar, en Slovénie, au Vietnam, en Ukraine, en Russie, en Chine, à Chypre, etc.

1 Arno Gruen, *La trahison du moi, pour devenir un être pleinement humain, autonome, authentique il importe d'accepter sa vulnérabilité* (1986), Paris 1991.
2 Shoshana Felman, *The Literary Speech Act. Don Juan with J. L. Austin, or Seduction in Two Languages*, Ithaca, NY 1983.
3 Judith Butler, *Trouble dans le genre. Le féminisme et la subversion de l'identité* (1990), Paris 2005.
4 Patricia Reinhart en entretien en novembre 2021.
5 Ibid.
6 Kaja Silverman, Harun Farocki, *Speaking about Godard*, New York 1998.
7 Patricia Reinhart en entretien en novembre 2021.
8 Virginia Woolf, *Une chambre à soi* (1929), Paris 1951.
9 Patricia Reinhart en entretien en novembre 2021.
10 Ibid.
11 Ibid.

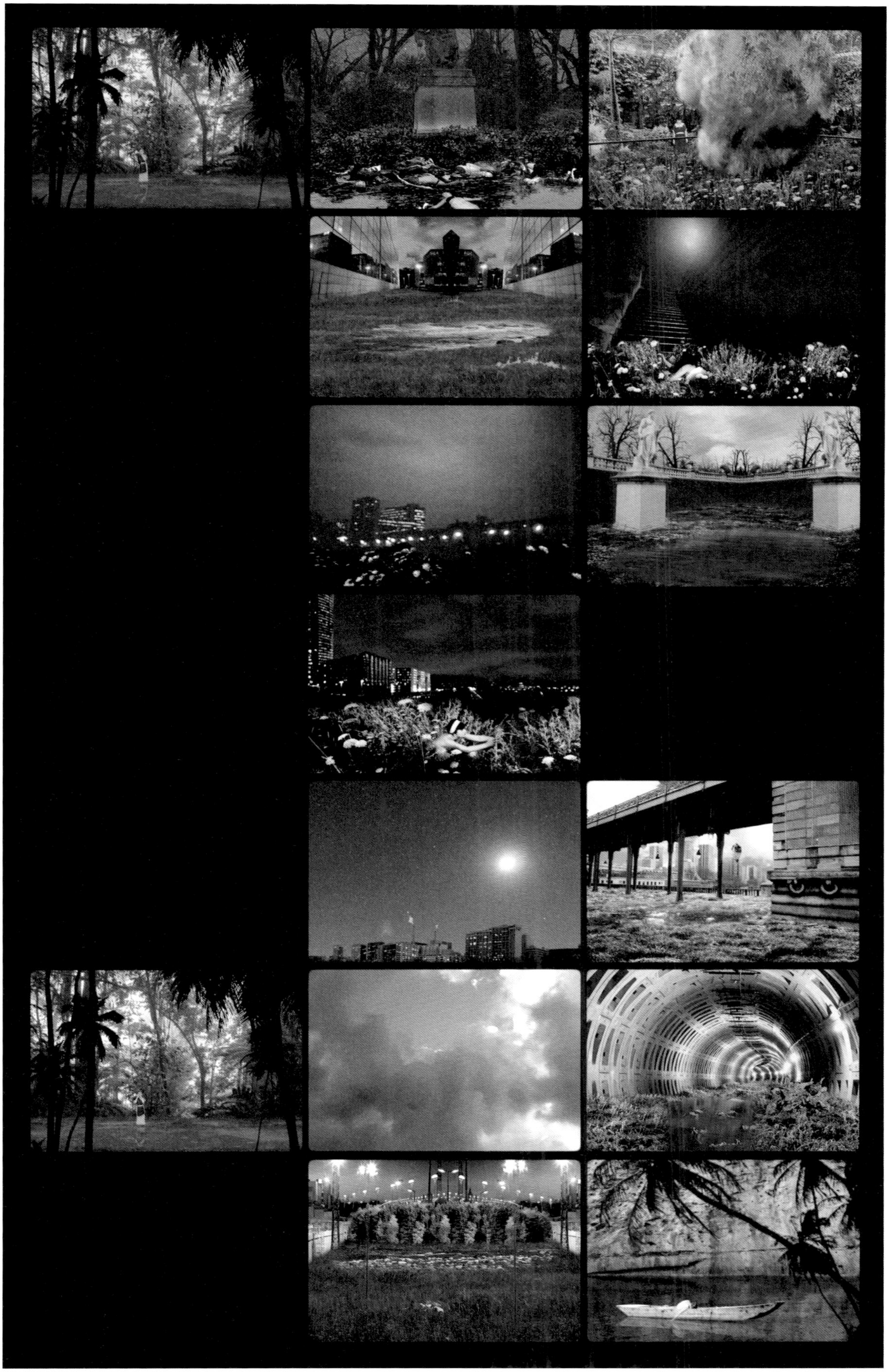

Ein Nachtstück, three-channel video installation, Ciné Collage, 2011/12

Patricia Reinhart

born 1977 in Vienna, Austria.
From 1995 until 2000 she studied painting at the Academy of Fine Arts, Vienna, Austria.
Master classes Wolfgang Hollegha, Sue Williams, Muntean/Rosenblum.
2000 she received her master degree with honours.
From 1999 to 2001 she studied acting at the Gustav Mahler Conservatory and in private lessons, Vienna, Austria.

geboren 1977 in Wien, Österreich.
Von 1995 bis 2000 studierte sie Malerei an der Akademie der bildenden Künste, Wien, Österreich.
Meisterklassen bei Wolfgang Hollegha, Sue Williams, Muntean/Rosenblum.
2000 Diplom mit Auszeichnung.
Von 1999 bis 2001 studierte sie Schauspiel am Gustav-Mahler-Konservatorium und im Privatunterricht, Wien, Österreich.

née en 1977 à Vienne, Autriche.
De 1995 à 2000, elle étudie la peinture à l'Académie des Beaux-Arts de Vienne, en Autriche,
chez Wolfgang Hollegha, Sue Williams, Muntean/Rosenblum.
En 2000, elle obtient sa maîtrise avec mention.
De 1999 à 2001, elle étudie le théâtre au Conservatoire Gustav Mahler et en cours privés, Vienne, Autriche.

Solo exhibitions · **Einzelausstellungen** · Expositions personnelles

2021 Flux / re.riddle / San Francisco, US
2019 In Bloom / Galerie Mansart / Paris, FR
2018 UNTITLED, ART Miami Beach / re.riddle / Miami Beach, US
2018 Nuit Blanche / Constellation de l'Île Saint-Louis / Paris, FR
2017 Berlin Art Week / Kanya Berlin Project Space / Berlin, DE
2016 Leucadian Leap / Rinomina / Paris, FR
2015 Les feux de l'amour / Galerie Günter Salzmann / Innsbruck, AT
2014 Synchronicity II / The Black Velvet Room / Paris, FR
2013 Ein Nachtstück / Cité internationale des arts / Paris, FR
2011 Avant de mourir / Galerie Lisa Ruyter / Vienna, AT
2008 Nocturne / Künstlerhaus – Passagegalerie / Vienna, AT
2008 The Silence was Vast / Galerie Dana Charkasi / Vienna, AT
2007 Lyda's Death / Oficina#1 / Caracas, VE
2006 Through Woods and Meadows / Galerie Dana Charkasi / Vienna, AT
2005 Trust Me / marks blond project / Sammlung Häuser und Wir / Zürich, CH
2004 I left Paris by a One Way Street / Brick–5 / Vienna, AT
2004 Flirt Me / marks blond project / Bern, CH
2004 My Neonline Paintings / Quelle / Vienna, AT
2003 *) / Daponte / Vienna, AT
2002 Träume ich noch immer? / Artothek – Galerie Alte Schmiede / Vienna, AT
2001 Ouvert / Cité internationale des arts / Paris, FR
2000 Untitled / Projectroom Muntean/Rosenblum / Vienna, AT
1999 Untitled / Kunsträume Vincent / Vienna, AT

Group exhibitions · **Gruppenausstellungen** · Expositions collectives

2020 Dust: The Plates of the Present / Centre Pompidou / Paris, FR
2020 Double Trouble / Galerie Mansart / Paris, FR
2019 The Body Electric / re.riddle / San Francisco, US
2019 Disrupting Identity / 5pace / Berlin, DE
2019 Quiet Days / Le31 / Paris, FR
2018 6+6 – Encounter #02 / PARALLEL VIENNA / Projektraum Viktor Eucher / Vienna, AT
2018 Polar Editions / Art-o-rama / Rinomina / Marseille, FR
2018 Uncanny Valley / curated by Francis Ruyter / Vin Vin / Vienna, AT
2018 INTOTO 6 / curated by Thomas Fougeirol, Pepo Salazar and Julien Careyn / Fondation d'entreprise Ricard / Paris, FR
2018 For One Night Only / La Sira / Asnières-sur-Seine, FR
2018 UNTITLED, ART San Francisco / re.riddle / San Francisco, US
2017 sommer.frische.kunst / Kraftwerk / Bad Gastein, AT
2016 Collective / curated by Bau Institute / FiveMyles / Brooklyn, NY, US
2016 My Castle is your Home / curated by Helga Schmidhuber / Nassauischer Kunstverein / Wiesbaden, DE
2015 Summer 15 / curated by Patricia Asbæk / CCA Kunsthalle / Mallorca, ES
2015 The Tears of Henry, James, Ernest, Lion, Arnold, Oskar and Alma / CCA Gallery / Mallorca, ES
2014 JUST ADD WATER! / Gallery Asbæk / Kopenhagen, DK
2014 48°28'39"N 2°12'47"E – Les pierres se battent entre elles / curated by Allison Somers and Emmanuelle Day / Auvers-Saint-Georges, FR
2014 Under The Bow / B-Side / Münster, DE
2014 JUST ADD WATER! / curated by Patricia Asbæk / CCA Kunsthalle / Mallorca, ES
2014 Scale Small Scale / Speicher II / Münster, DE
2014 Ici & lá / Cité internationale des arts / Paris, FR
2013 Nuit Blanche / curated by Lowave / Perle / Paris, FR
2013 Mondes parallèles / Église St. Merry / Paris, FR
2012 Predicting Memories / Vienna Art Week / curated by Ursula Maria Probst and Robert Punkenhofer / K. K. Telegrafenamt / Vienna, AT
2011 Human Frames / curated by Silke Schmickl / Kunst im Tunnel / Düsseldorf, DE
2010 Women / kerstin engholm galerie / Vienna, AT
2008 AUSTRIA conTEMPORARY / Essl Museum / Klosterneuburg, AT
2008 Bologna Chicks / marks blond project / Bern, CH
2008 Anton Faistauer Award / Galerie im Traklhaus / Salzburg, AT
2007 VIENNAFAIR / Galerie Dana Charkasi / Vienna, AT
2006 Preview Berlin / Galerie Dana Charkasi / Berlin, DE
2006 3 Generations – 3 Regions / Art Collection of the City of Vienna / Burg Schlaining / Schlaining, AT
2005 marks blond holidays / marks blond project / Biennale / Prague, CZ
2005 ART|36|BASEL / Galerie Scalo / Basel, CH
2005 Before Summer / Atelier Quelle / Vienna, AT
2005 Black is Beautiful / marks blond project / Whitespace / Zürich, CH
2005 Flexibition #4. Sehensucht / Galerie Hatsov / Vienna, AT
2004 Cart Zürich – marks blond goes out / marks blond project / Zürich, CH
2004 Book + Portfolio / Betonsalon / Paris, FR
2003 Pfann Ohmann Award / Künstlerhaus / Vienna, AT
2000 Diplomarbeiten / Semperdepot / Academy of Fine Arts / Vienna, AT
1998 Drawings / Kupferstichkabinett / Vienna, AT
1998 Spices & Diversities & Academies / curated by Harald Szeemann / Academy of Fine Arts / Vienna, AT

Collections · **Sammlungen** · Collections

Centre Pompidou / Paris, FR
Albertina / Vienna, AT
Bibliothèque nationale de France / Paris, FR
CCA Andratx – Center for Contemporary Art / Mallorca, ES
Ursula Blickle Video Archiv – Belvedere / Vienna, AT
Gesellschaft der Freunde der bildenden Kunst / Vienna, AT
Federal Ministry for the Arts, AT
City of Vienna, AT
Private Collections

Honours · **Auszeichnungen** · Honneurs

2018 International Scholarship / Artist in Residence / CCA Andratx – Center for Contemporary Art, ES
2017 International Scholarship / Artist in Residence / sommer.frische.kunst – Bad Gastein, AT
2015 BAU Institute Arts Residency Award / BAU Institute, US
2015 International Scholarship / Artist in Residence / CCA Andratx – Center for Contemporary Art, ES
2013 Studio Scholarship at the Cité internationale des arts Paris / Photography and Video / Federal Ministry for Education, Arts and Culture, AT
2012 International Scholarship / Artist in Residence / CCA Andratx – Center for Contemporary Art, ES
2011 Austrian State Grant for Fine Art / Federal Ministry for Education, Arts and Culture, AT
2009 Nomination Strabag Art Award / Strabag Kunstforum, Vienna, AT
2008 Nomination Anton Faistauer Award / Galerie im Traklhaus, Salzburg, AT
2003 Nomination Pfann Ohmann Award / Künstlerhaus, Vienna, AT
2001 Studio Scholarship at the Cité internationale des arts Paris / Painting / Federal Ministry for Education, Arts and Culture, AT
1998 Master School Award of the Academy of Fine Arts Vienna, AT

Grants · **Stipendien** · Bourses

2021 Scholarship for a catalogue production of the Federal Ministry for Arts, Culture, the Civil Service and Sport, AT
2021 Scholarship for a catalogue production of the Cultural Department of the City of Vienna, AT
2021 Scholarship for a catalogue production by Bildrecht, AT
2020 Fellowship from the CNAP – Centre national des arts plastiques, FR
2019 Scholarship for Venice of the Federal Ministry for Education, Arts and Culture, AT
2018 Scholarship for the US of the Federal Ministry for Education, Arts and Culture, AT
2018 Scholarship for Paris of the Federal Ministry for Education, Arts and Culture, AT
2018 Fellowship of the Forum Culturel Autrichien, Austrian Embassy/BMEIA, Paris, FR
2014 Scholarship for a catalogue production of the Federal Ministry for Education, Arts and Culture, AT
2013 Scholarship for Paris of the Federal Ministry for Education, Arts and Culture, AT
2012 Scholarship for Mallorca of the Federal Ministry for Education, Arts and Culture, AT
2007 Scholarship for Venezuela of the Federal Ministry for Education, Arts and Culture, AT
2006 Scholarship for Paris of the Federal Ministry for Education, Arts and Culture, AT
2002 Fellowship of the Emanuel and Sophie Fohn Foundation, AT
2001 Fellowship of the Emanuel and Sophie Fohn Foundation, AT
1999 Fellowship of the Academy of Fine Arts Vienna, AT

Artist residences · **Künstlerresidenzen** · Résidences d'artistes

2018 CCA Andratx / Mallorca, ES
2017 sommer.frische.kunst / Bad Gastein, AT
2015 BAU Institute @ The Camargo Foundation / Cassis, FR
2015 CCA Andratx / Mallorca, ES
2014 Cité internationale des arts / Paris, FR
2013 Cité internationale des arts / Paris, FR
2012 CCA Andratx / Mallorca, ES
2010 Cité internationale des arts / Paris, FR
2006 Cité internationale des arts / Paris, FR
2001 Cité internationale des arts / Paris, FR

Vinyls · **Vinylplatten** · Vinyles

2014 *Composition in D minor (pour lui)*, piece for a piano, Paris, FR / composed and arranged by Patricia Reinhart / 7'00'', A + B, limited edition
2003 *Untitled (Chanson d'Hélène)*, recorded session with artists and musicians at Quelle / voice: Patricia Reinhart, Atelier Quellenstraße Vienna, AT / 5'23'', A + B, limited edition

Screenings · **Filmprojektionen** · Projections

2020 In Kepler's Gardens / re.riddle / Ars Electronica / Linz, AT
2018 Nuit Blanche / Constellation de l'Île Saint-Louis / Paris, FR
2018 Nuit Blanche / Constellation des Invalides / FICEP / Paris, FR
2017 Berlin Art Week / Kanya Berlin Project Space / Berlin, DE
2015 Synchronicity IV / The Camargo Foundation / Cassis, FR
2015 Synchronicity III / Same Same Beach / Cassis, FR
2014 Rencontres Internationales / Haus der Kulturen der Welt / Berlin, DE
2014 Synchronicity I / Canal Saint-Martin / Paris, FR
2014 Rencontres Internationales / Gaité Lyrique and Palais de Tokyo / Paris, FR
2013 Nuit Blanche / curated by Lowave / Perle / Paris, FR
2013 La Société de Curiosités / curated by Silke Schmickl / La Société de Curiosités / Paris, FR
2013 Ein Nachtstück / Cité internationale des arts / Paris, FR
2012 Human Frames / curated by Silke Schmickl / Werkstatt der Kulturen / Berlin, DE
2012 Poèmes / Cala Llamp / Mallorca, ES
2011 Human Frames / curated by Silke Schmickl / The Substitution, Singapore, SG / Kunst im Tunnel, Düsseldorf, DE
2010 700IS Reindeerland / Video Festival / IS, NO, US, HU, UK, PT
2008 An den Grenzen der Begriffe – Arbeiten mit der Filmkamera / curated by Günter Puller / Filmfestival Bayreuth, DE / Topkino, Vienna, AT / General Public, Berlin, DE
2007 Lyda's Death / Oficina#1, Playa Grande / Choroni, VE
2005 Black is Beautiful / marks blond project @ Whitespace / Zürich, CH
2003 Matchcuts / Votiv 21 / Vienna, AT
2002 Super 8 – Festival / Paris, FR

Film work · **Filme** · Filmographie

2017 *Anoir and the Woman in the Garden* / Ciné Collage, HD Video, sound / 9'47'', 3 + 1 AP, ES/FR
2014 *Die ihr Brot mit Tränen aß (Requiem for an Unendurable Paradise)* / single-channel video installation, vinyl and record player / Ciné Collage, sound / 5'45'', 3 + 1 AP, ES/FR
2014 *Le Radeau de la Méduse* / Ciné Collage, no sound / 0'24'', 3 + 1 AP, FR
2012 *Ein Nachtstück* / three-channel video installation / Ciné Collage, no sound / 5'00'', 3 + 1 AP, FR/AT
2011 *13 Poèmes visibles (Ophélia & Avant de mourir)* / Ciné Collage and Super-8 film, no sound / 0'08''–0'35'', 5 + 2 AP, HU/AT
2008 *Nocturne in Black* / Ciné Collage, sound / 3'22'', 3 + 1 AP, AT / courtesy: the artist and Albertina, Vienna, AT
2008 *Kirkirerland* / Ciné Collage and Super-8 film, no sound / 1'10'', 5 + 2 AP, AT / courtesy: the artist, Bibliothèque nationale de France, Paris, FR, and Ursula Blickle Video Archiv – Belvedere, Vienna, AT
2007 *4. Akt Lyda's Death* / Ciné Collage, sound / 3'50'', 3 + 1 AP, AT
2006 *Untitled/Silentmovie* / Ciné Collage, sound / 3'00'', 3 + 1 AP, AT
2006 *Der bittere Beigeschmack* / Ciné Collage, sound / 3'00'', 3 + 1 AP, AT
2005 *Heroes & Loser* / Ciné Collage, sound / 3'00'', 3 + 1 AP, AT
2004 *The Adventures of Rick Castle and Santa Fee* / Ciné Collage, sound / 2'30'', 3 + 1 AP, AT
2004 *Paris mon amour* / Ciné Collage, sound / 3'00'', 3 + 1 AP, AT
2004 *Die Sonne meines Lebens* / Ciné Collage, sound / 3'12'', 3 + 1 AP, AT
2004 *Zug* / Ciné Collage, sound / 1'30'', 3 + 1 AP, AT
2004 *Barbara & Paul* / Ciné Collage, sound / 2'30'', 3 + 1 AP, AT
2004 *Blindness* / DV, sound / 3'00'', 3 + 1 AP, AT
2004 *Triple Tak* / Ciné Collage, sound / 4'30'', 3 + 1 AP, AT
2004 *Fight* / DV, sound / 1'00'', 3 + 1 AP, AT
2004 *Something's Stilling* / DV, sound / 3'30'', 3 + 1 AP, AT
2004 *Depeche Mode Dancer* / DV, sound / 2'30'', 3 + 1 AP, AT
2003 *Kanikula* / DV, sound / 7'00'', 3 + 1 AP, HU/AT
2003 *Chercher le destin* / DV, sound / 7'00'', 3 + 1 AP, FR/AT
2002 *A.M.* / Super-8 film and DV, sound, 8'00'', 1 + 1 AP, AT
2001 *Pont Neuf* / Super-8 film, no sound, 3'20'', 1 AP, FR
2001 *Pigalle* / Super-8 film, no sound, 3'20'', 1 AP, FR
2001 *Métro* / Super-8 film, no sound, 3'20'', 1 AP, FR

Imprint
Impressum
Colophon

Texts · Texte · Textes
Synne Genzmer, Ursula Maria Probst, Barbara Rüdiger

Translations · **Übersetzungen** · Traductions
Morwenna Coquelin, Nikolay Hersey

Editing · **Lektorat** · Lektorat
German / Deutsch / Allemand: textstern/Ulrike Ritter
Englisch / Englisch / Anglais: Barbara Stanzl
French / Französisch / Français: Julia Walter, Renée Zachariou

Graphic Design · **Graphische Gestaltung** · Conception graphique
Katharina Gattermann

Photo Credits · **Fotonachweis** · Crédits photos
Patricia Reinhart
Daniela Beranek (p. 5–14; p. 17–19; p. 21–24; p. 27–51)

Image Editing · **Bildbearbeitung** · Traitement d'images
Daniela Beranek, Katharina Gattermann, Pixelstorm/Manfred Kostal
Font · **Schrift** · Police de caractères
Soleil by Wolfang Homola, TypeTogether
Paper · **Papier** · Papier
Munken Lynx, Arctic Volume White
Printed by · **Druck** · Imprimé par
Holzhausen Druck GmbH

www.patriciareinhart.com

Printed in Austria · **Gedruckt in Österreich** · Imprimé en Autriche

ISBN 978-3-903572-91-1

Published by · **Erschienen im** · Publié par
VfmK Verlag für moderne Kunst GmbH, Vienna · Wien · Vienne, AT
www.vfmk.org

Distribution · **Vertrieb** · Distribution
Europe, LKG, www.lkg-va.de
UK: Cornerhouse Publications, www.cornerhousepublications.org
USA: D.A.P., www.artbook.com

The Deutsche Nationalbibliothek lists this publication in the Deutsche Nationalbibliografie; detailed bibliographic data is available in the Internet at dnb.de. · Die Deutsche Nationalbibliothek verzeichnet diese Publikation in der Deutschen Nationalbibliografie; detaillierte bibliografische Daten sind im Internet über dnb.de abrufbar. · La Deutsche Nationalbibliothek répertorie cette publication dans la Deutsche Nationalbibliografie ; des données bibliographiques détaillées sont disponibles sur le site Internet dnb.de.

This publication has been made possible through the support of the Arts and Culture division of the Federal Chancellery of Austria, the City of Vienna and Bildrecht. · Diese Publikation wurde ermöglicht durch die Unterstützung der Kunst- und Kulturabteilung des Bundeskanzleramtes Österreich, der Stadt Wien und Bildrecht. · Cette publication a été rendue possible grâce au soutien de la Division des Arts et de la Culture de la Chancellerie fédérale autrichienne, de la Ville de Vienne et de Bildrecht.

My heartfelt gratitude goes to my family, all friends and supporters.
Mein herzlicher Dank gilt meiner Familie, allen Freund:innen und Unterstützer:innen.
Mes remerciements les plus sincères vont à ma famille, à tous mes amis et à tous ceux qui me soutiennent.

Gabriela Anco, Patricia and Jacob Asbæk, Daniela Baldelli, Daniela Beranek, Julia Bromirski, Dana Charkasi, Valentina Cipullo, Morwenna Coquelin, Emmanuelle Day, Carine Dolek, Sonja Engelhardt, Thomas Fougeirol, Julia Frey, Joachim Lothar Gartner, Katharina Gattermann, Synne Genzmer, Mathias Georgi, Gerhard Gleich, Andrea von Goetz und Schwanenfliess, Virpi Helen, Jackie Herbst, Wolfgang Hollegha, Candace Huey, Silvia Jaklitsch, Walter Keller, Iona Kleinhaut, Günther Kleinpeter, Jean-Yves Langlais, Xuwon Lee, Marie Lemarchand, Markus Lichti, Karine Llorenz, Lauren Luloff, Florian Mair, Frédéric D. Oberland, Ursula Maria Probst, Günter Puller, Patricia Reinhart-Faessler, Ulrike Ritter, Barbara Rüdiger, Francis Ruyter, Alice Schneider, Silke Schmickl, Radwina Saga Seiler, Allison Somers, Judith Stehlik, Daniel Suter, Jo-ey Tang, Sue Williams

Bildrecht · Stadt Wien · Bundeskanzleramt